ONE FAIR WAGE

Also by Saru Jayaraman

The New Urban Immigrant Workforce

Behind the Kitchen Door

Forked: A New Standard for American Dining

Bite Back: People Taking on Corporate Food and Winning
(with Kathryn De Master)

ONE FAIR WAGE

ENDING SUBMINIMUM PAY IN AMERICA

SARU JAYARAMAN

NEW YORK
LONDON

Requests for permission to reproduce selections from this book should be made
through our website: https://thenewpress.com/contact.

Published in the United States by The New Press, New York, 2021
Distributed by Two Rivers Distribution

ISBN 978-1-62097-533-6 (hc)
ISBN 978-1-62097-534-3 (ebook)
CIP data is available

The New Press publishes books that promote and enrich public discussion and
understanding of the issues vital to our democracy and to a more equitable world.
These books are made possible by the enthusiasm of our readers; the support of a
committed group of donors, large and small; the collaboration of our many partners
in the independent media and the not-for-profit sector; booksellers, who often
hand-sell New Press books; librarians; and above all by our authors.

www.thenewpress.com

Book design and composition by Bookbright Media
This book was set in Bembo and Electra

Printed in the United States of America

2 4 6 8 10 9 7 5 3 1

Dedicated to service workers and all working people unjustly paid subminimum, subhuman wages, with the hope that all shall be valued as the skilled professionals that they are

Contents

ONE FAIR WAGE

Introduction

Jaime started working in Virginia Beach restaurants as a teenager. She worked at a sports bar earning $2.13 an hour plus tips—the federal subminimum wage for tipped workers. As a Black person, she encountered countless acts of racism. "They didn't want me to serve them; they'd request a different server. Sometimes they wouldn't ask for a different server, but they wouldn't want me to touch anything on their plate. If the kitchen made a mistake with the food, they'd assume it was because I was too dumb to get it right." As a woman, sexual harassment was the rule, not the exception. "It was super common for the customers and the male staff to put their hands in your pocket, to grab you. If you didn't flirt with them, they'd complain to the manager, and then you'd get in trouble. Then you get the sh*tty section, and you'd have to go work somewhere else. Since we don't get paid an actual wage, we have to go somewhere you can get tips."[1]

At one point, that "somewhere else to get tips" became New York City. Jaime put all her belongings in a U-Haul, drove up to New York, and lived in the truck until her first restaurant job brought in enough to allow her to get a place to live. When she landed a fine dining restaurant server position in midtown Manhattan, she was hopeful that she would not face the same kind of racism and sexual harassment she faced in Virginia, until one day her Southern general manager revealed it was no different in New York City. "I was asking to switch shifts with another server, and he put his finger to his temple and said, 'I don't want to listen to your mammy whining.'" Jaime complained to Human Resources, which claimed to not know that the derogatory "mammy" term harkens back to slavery. The manager was never reprimanded in any way. Like so many other workers, Jaime moved on to another restaurant, continuously searching for a company that would respect her dignity and professionalism. All of that was before the pandemic.

After eight years of working as a server and bartender in New York City, Jaime's life—and the life of everyone on the globe—was upended by the COVID-19 pandemic. Laid off with the rest of her staff in March 2020, Jamie heard little from her employers until July, when she received a letter mandating that she return to work. There were no questions regarding COVID or whether she was sick or at risk, only that she must return or face termination of her unemployment insurance benefits.

Jaime had numerous concerns about going back to work, from fears about her health and safety to worries about how she would pay bills at a time when tips were so dramatically reduced, capacity was limited, and customers were still infrequent. She knew, however, that she did not have a real choice.

"If I could collect unemployment benefits and stay safe, I would. But we have to accept their terms of employment or lose unemployment benefits," says Jaime. This was especially true for tipped workers, who were lucky if they received unemployment insurance benefits; 60 percent reported experiencing great challenges accessing benefits because the state told them their wages were too low to meet the minimum threshold to qualify.[2]

Jaime's restaurant's reopening coincided with a surge in national uprisings for racial equity after the murder of George Floyd. As a Black woman, Jaime was frustrated and disheartened by the complete lack of care and communication on the part of her employer to address either the pandemic or rising calls for an end to anti-Black racism. As a server and bartender, this lack of care was compounded by the fact that her livelihood was completely dependent on pleasing customers at all costs to obtain tips. Within the first couple weeks of reopening, customers were starting to show severe resistance and hostility toward restaurant staff. In one instance, a customer refused to wear a mask despite being repeatedly asked by service staff. One of Jaime's coworkers was forced to de-escalate the situation and the irate customer eventually left. As he was leaving, the customer yelled that the service staff represented what was wrong with America, and that if he wanted to risk his life that was his choice. He expressly stated that he would be voting for Trump come November.

This incident was not Jaime's first encounter with coded racism and harassment on the part of customers or management in the restaurant industry. For tipped workers like Jaime, the customer is always right; the customer pays your bills, not the employer, and as a result, the customer's biases dictate a worker's livelihood. In fact, Black women in restaurant dining earn $8 less an hour than their white men counterparts in New York because they earn less in tips— both because they are segregated into more casual restaurants, where tips are smaller, and because even in fine dining restaurants, customer bias results in workers of color earning less in tips.[3] Jaime has seen coworkers fired over racist Yelp reviews left by customers.

Thousands of Jaime's peers have reported that hostility and harassment toward tipped workers dramatically increased during the pandemic, even as these same workers were being asked to do more for less. Suddenly tipped workers were being asked to enforce social distancing and mask rules—serving as public health marshals in highly dangerous settings—when workers reported tips were down 50 to 75 percent.[4] Worst of all, thousands of Jaime's peers have reported that sexual harassment increased during the pandemic. Hundreds of women have reported that male customers asked them to remove their masks so that they could judge their looks and determine their tips on that basis. The phenomenon became so prevalent that it earned its own hashtag: #MaskualHarassment.

During the pandemic, restaurant workers became one of the only essential workers to not receive a full minimum wage, and the only essential workers to be asked to remove their protective gear for the chance to earn their income.

Jaime is not sure she will stay in the restaurant industry. "I take pride in the education and knowledge I've gained over the last fifteen years. Not everyone can be a fine dining server. The only thing that makes me not want to be in this industry is the way I'm treated at work and treated by guests. If I were given actual paid time off and benefits like other professionals—if I were given a living wage, it would be so much different. We get paid because of our smiles, intellect, and charm. The state does not require our employer to pay us . . . that's the sh*tty part of the industry. . . . It's paid my rent and bills, put me through school, but I've worked really hard, and I've been put in compromising positions on lots of occasions. I shouldn't have had men put hands in my pocket or ask me what I'm doing after work, or if I can work in their home. I should be protected from that."

Jaime and her coworkers have been organizing for increased racial equity in her current restaurant, but she knows that larger transformation needs to happen at the legislative level. In January 2021, then President-Elect Biden announced that he would include a $15 minimum wage and One Fair Wage—a full minimum wage for tipped workers, with tips on top—in his $1.9 trillion COVID-19 stimulus legislative package. For Jaime and so many others, the change could not have come soon enough. "The tipping system is antiquated and feeds into the idea that we should be grateful for everything that we get. Employers benefit from the fact that we have to serve customers, sometimes nonconsensually, for our wages, instead of getting our wages directly from our employer."

Starting on March 16, 2020, over six million restaurant and other tipped service workers nationwide—including nail salon and car wash workers, parking attendants, gig workers, and more—lost their jobs as a result of the COVID-19 pandemic. For most low-wage workers across the economy, the shutdown meant the loss of their wages; for tipped workers, it meant the loss of both wages and tips. Even worse, because of the enormous fluctuations in tips and challenges with reporting them as income, about 60 percent of these tipped workers were denied unemployment insurance benefits by their states. In many cases, they were told that because they earned the subminimum wage for tipped workers, allowed in forty-three states nationwide, they earned too little to qualify for benefits that they had paid taxes to obtain. Some of these workers were able to obtain federal unemployment insurance benefits, which was not based on a measurement of prior income, but even then it was severely delayed and then stopped by the federal government, leaving millions in an extremely dire situation.

When some of these workers were called back to work,

they were asked to return for a subminimum wage with tips that are reported to be 50 to 75 percent lower than they were before. This left tipped workers with an impossible choice: go back to work and risk exposure to the coronavirus for a subminimum wage with very little guarantee of tips, or refuse such a job and lose any unemployment insurance benefits they may have obtained.

Prior to the pandemic, there were 13.6 million restaurant workers and nearly 6 million tipped workers across the United States, including restaurant, car wash, nail salon, tech platform delivery, and other workers.[5] The National Restaurant Association had argued since Emancipation that, given customer tips, they should be able to pay their tipped employees a subminimum wage, today just $2.13 an hour federally. A legacy of slavery, the subminimum wage for tipped workers today is a gender equity issue; 70 percent of tipped workers are women, disproportionately women of color, who work in nail and hair salons and casual restaurants like IHOP and Denny's, live in poverty at three times the rate of the rest of the U.S. workforce, and suffer from the worst sexual harassment of any industry because they are forced to tolerate inappropriate customer behavior in order to feed their families in tips.[6]

Seven states—California, Oregon, Washington, Alaska, Minnesota, Nevada, and Montana—have rejected this legacy of slavery and pay One Fair Wage—a full minimum wage with tips on top. These states have comparable or higher restaurant sales per capita, job growth among tipped workers and the restaurant industry overall, and tipping averages than the forty-three states with lower wages for tipped workers, and half the rate of sexual harassment in the restaurant industry.[7] One Fair Wage, the organization I lead, has been fighting to ensure that the nation follows the leadership of these seven states.

The subminimum wage for tipped workers resulted in a horrific experience for millions of tipped workers as a result of the COVID-19 economic shutdown. As mentioned above, most were ineligible for unemployment insurance benefits; thousands of tipped workers have reported to us that they faced tremendous challenges in obtaining unemployment insurance benefits because their subminimum wage plus tips is so low it does not meet the minimum threshold to obtain unemployment insurance benefits. In other words, these workers were penalized because their employers paid them too little. Even among those who were eligible, unemployment insurance benefits were calculated based on the subminimum wage plus, generally, an underevaluation of their tips. Millions of workers find themselves now unable to pay for rent, food for their children, or other bills.

The consequences of the racial inequality that has long been documented in the restaurant industry became painfully clear. Workers of color were disproportionately denied unemployment insurance benefits because they were more likely than white workers to have worked in casual restaurants where they received their tips in cash, and state unemployment insurance systems automatically denied these workers because their incomes appear to be too low to meet the minimum threshold to qualify.[8]

Tipped workers are the largest workforce allowed to be paid a subminimum wage in the United States, but they are by no means the only workforce allowed to be paid a subminimum wage, and they're not even the only workforce for whom the subminimum wage is a legacy of slavery.[9] Incarcerated workers may be paid a subminimum wage as little as 11 cents an hour or $1 a day, depending on the state, due to the exception to the Thirteenth Amendment that allows for slavery in the case of incarceration. Workers with disabilities may be paid a subminimum wage based on decades of law allowing employers to segregate workers with disabilities into "sheltered workshops," or separate and wholly unequal workplaces. Youth may be paid a subminimum wage in multiple states based on an antiquated notion that youth are not supporting families. And gig workers, growing by the thousands, may be paid the equivalent of a subminimum wage because they are misclassified as independent contractors. In total, all subminimum wage workers make up more than one-tenth of the American workforce.[10]

In 2019, our campaign for One Fair Wage grew from representing tipped subminimum wage workers to include all subminimum wage workers, calling for "No Worker Left Behind." We advance the idea that no one who works in the United States should be paid less than the minimum wage—after all, what else does "minimum" refer to if so many millions of workers can be paid less?

"Take Off Your Mask So I Know How Much to Tip You": Health and Harassment Experiences of Service Workers During COVID-19

In fall 2020, hundreds of thousands of these workers started to be called back to work as indoor dining began. Many workers reported that they would have liked to refuse these jobs due to having a pre-existing condition or living with family members who were at high risk of contracting or dying from the virus; these workers knew that restaurants are particularly high-risk environments, but they could not refuse the work as they would have lost their unemployment insurance benefits or opportunity to return to their job later, leaving them without any income. The CDC confirmed these workers' fears when it reported in September 2020 that adults were twice as likely to obtain the virus after eating in a restaurant.[11]

But the CDC's findings were a warning not only to restaurant workers—they were actually a study of restaurant consumers. With restaurants becoming a source of spread among all people, food service workers became essential workers and de facto public health marshals, enforcing critical mask and social distancing protocols in one of the most dangerous environments in terms of spread of the pandemic. Unfortunately, unlike all other essential workers, they were not routinely guaranteed a standard minimum wage and thus lived at the mercy of customers' tips.

In the fall of 2020 we conducted a survey of 1,675 workers who had returned to work; the responses demonstrated that workers were being subjected to shockingly high rates of exposure to the virus and increased sexual harassment, all while working for a subminimum wage and vastly reduced tips. Nearly half (44 percent) of workers reported that at least one or more of the employees in their restaurant had contracted COVID-19. Most workers (84 percent) reported being within six feet of at least one person who was not wearing a mask in every shift, and more than one-third (33 percent) reported being within six feet of thirty or more maskless individuals on every shift. Over 80 percent of workers (83 percent) reported that their tips have declined during COVID-19, and nearly two-thirds (66 percent) reported that their tips have declined at least 50 percent.[12]

If the increased risk for lower pay was not bad enough, workers reported severely increased customer hostility and harassment during the pandemic. Over three-quarters of workers (78 percent) reported experiencing or witnessing hostile behavior from customers in response to staff enforcing COVID-19 safety protocols, and nearly 60 percent (59 percent) reported experiencing such hostility at least weekly. As a result, over half of workers (58 percent) reported feeling reluctant to enforce COVID-19 protocols out of concern that customers would tip them less. Indeed, two-thirds of workers (67 percent) reported having received a lesser tip after enforcing COVID-19 protocols on customers, usually on a frequent basis. The survey results demonstrated that workers' vulnerability and dependence on tips, rather than receiving a full minimum wage, prevents them from serving as the public health marshals we expect them to be.[13]

Most shockingly, more than 40 percent of workers (41 percent) reported that there was a noticeable change in the frequency of unwanted sexualized comments from customers, and just over one-quarter (25 percent) reported that they had experienced or witnessed a significant change in the frequency of such sexual harassment. Nearly 250 workers shared sexualized comments from customers, a substantial portion of which were a request from male customers that women servers remove their mask so that they could judge their looks and determine their tips on that basis. Many comments were even worse, such as "Pull that mask down so I can see if I want to take you home later," and "Take off your mask so I can stick my tongue down your throat." In other words, women were being asked to expose themselves to the virus—and potentially to death—for the sexual pleasure of male customers. They were some of the only essential workers who were not paid a minimum wage and were being asked to remove their protective gear in order to earn their base wages. The subminimum wage thus changed from being an issue of racial, gender, and economic justice to becoming an issue of life or death.[14]

Shaping Relief to Reshape the Future

The pandemic revealed the dysfunction of subminimum wages in the United States. As a result, we were able to expand our fight for One Fair Wage for all workers, and to push our fight for One Fair Wage with increased urgency. We organized strikes around the country; we launched the One Fair Wage Emergency Fund on March 16, 2020, to provide cash relief to thousands of low-wage service workers; we also provided individual counseling to workers with regard to their unemployment benefits and finances. But we also understood that the answer to such fundamental challenges lay in government action. We organized thousands of workers into large national and state tele-town halls and virtual rallies with congressmembers, governors, and other state legislators to allow them to raise their voices and make demands. It was a new and unique moment in organizing—thousands of workers attended these virtual events and demanded change with a fervor we've rarely seen, in which they demanded that they receive One Fair Wage before they go back to work.

All of these efforts culminated in January 2021, when then

President-Elect Biden announced that he would include the Raise the Wage Act, which proposes a $15 minimum wage and a multiyear phasing out of the subminimum wage for tipped workers, youth, and workers with disabilities, in his $1.9 trillion COVID-19 stimulus bill. And while it did not end up in that stimulus package, the Raise the Wage Act has gained tremendous traction as a standalone bill in Congress. So, while a subminimum wage for tipped workers and workers with disabilities remains in forty-three states, it is on its way out. And while we have to keep fighting to make sure no worker in America—tipped, disabled, incarcerated, gig, or anyone else—receives a subminimum wage, workers have already won huge, historic gains through their collective action during a global pandemic.

COVID-19 has revealed the deep structural inequities of the service sector, and has created a tremendous opportunity to organize both workers and employers for the change we always needed. There is no going back—we can only go forward together, and reimagine an economy in which all thrive.

1

The History of Subminimum Wages

The similar and intertwined histories of different categories of subminimum wage workers all reflect a common pattern: the historical devaluation of certain groups of people as being subhuman based on their identity.

The Subminimum Wage for Tipped Workers

The subminimum wage for tipped workers in this country is a direct legacy of slavery.

The practice of tipping originated in feudal Europe, where aristocrats and nobles provided tips as an extra or bonus on top of wages to their inferiors—the monetary embodiment of *noblesse oblige*. Tipping came to the United States in the mid-1850s, brought by aristocratic wealthy Americans seeking to emulate their European peers, but most Americans resoundingly rejected tipping as a vestige of feudalism and an anathema to democracy. At the time, waiters, who were mostly men, received an actual wage from their employers. In the mid-1850s, male waiters staged various restaurant workers' strikes across the country.[1] The strikes had mixed success. Some employers raised their wages, but many others were simply fired, replacing the waiters with women.[2]

After Emancipation in 1863, however, tipping spread rapidly as employers in the hospitality sector hired newly freed slaves as servers, porters, and hosts across the country. They refused to pay them a wage, forcing them to rely entirely on tips from customers.[3] While many other sectors also ended up adopting the notion of tips as wage replacement, the hospitality sector led the way in mutating the original concept of tips from being an extra or bonus on top of a wage to having tips become the wage itself—as a direct legacy of slavery. In this way, just as women and Black people entered the workforce in large numbers, the wage went down from an actual wage to zero. Thus, the subminimum wage for tipped workers cannot be understood as anything other than a devaluation of Black lives and women's work—one of the first instances of legalized gender pay inequity.

Two sectors of hospitality were impacted by this mutated notion of tips. First, the Pullman Company, a luxury train company, hired former slaves as porters and dining car waiters with an expectation of servility to white patrons who would tip them in lieu of wages.[4] In response, Black Pullman workers formed the Brotherhood of Sleeping Car Porters, the first Black union in the United States, which won the right to a guaranteed wage. Unfortunately, restaurant workers were not so fortunate. Freed slaves who moved north were refused employment in the skilled trades they had learned as slaves, and as a result, they were forced to become cooks, porters, and waiters entirely dependent on tips. Lobbying by industry groups sealed this arrangement—these were the predecessors to the National Restaurant Association (the "Other NRA," as advocates call it), the current behemoth trade lobby representing the interests of corporate restaurant chains.[5] By 1880, 43 percent of all workers employed in hotels and restaurants were African Americans.[6] In 1900, thirty-seven years after Emancipation, a quarter of all Black workers engaged in nonagricultural labor were employed as servants and waiters. Nearly three-quarters of these workers were women.[7] The feminization of the industry had begun some years prior; in 1850, a mostly-male workforce of waiters staged a national strike to increase their wages—which existed prior to Emancipation as a full wage before tips—and employers in Boston, New York, and Philadelphia replaced these male waiters with women in response to the strike.[8] In this way, many restaurants became majority female just before the introduction of the notion of a non-wage or subminimum wage for tipped workers was introduced.

The prevalence of Black workers in service occupations coincided with some efforts to eliminate tipping in the early 1900s. Several states enacted such bans, but many of these efforts had sharply disparate racial impacts. In 1910 in Washington, DC, Congress passed a law under which any restaurant waiter who accepted tips would be fined $500.

According to sources at the time, all restaurant waiters in the city were Black.[9] By 1926 the restaurant industry lobby, with the assistance of the courts, was able to roll back all of the tipping bans that had been enacted and was able to once again have employees depend completely on tips without wages.[10] During that same period, and with the advent of World War I, white women entered the restaurant workforce in large numbers and women quickly grew to become a majority of all servers. By 1940, nearly 70 percent of servers were women, dependent on tips for their income.[11]

When the Fair Labor Standards Act—a key piece of New Deal legislation—passed in 1938, it gave many workers the right to a minimum wage for the first time. However, the law excluded large groups of workers of color—including domestic workers, farmworkers, and tipped workers—who at the time were servers, bussers, porters, and bartenders, but also elevator operators and shoe shiners. While farmworkers and domestic workers had other restrictions placed on their wages, tipped workers in particular were told that they could be paid no wage as long as tips brought them to the full minimum wage. From 1938 until 1991, the federal minimum wage for tipped workers rose from $0 an hour to $2.13 an hour. Thanks to lobbying from the National Restaurant Association, it was frozen at $2.13 an hour in 1996 and has not risen since then.

In 2021, the nation's fastest-growing workforce can still be paid as little as $2.13 an hour.

Today, individual states may establish a minimum wage that is higher than the federal government's. This has resulted in a patchwork of state policies in which restaurant workers in sixteen states receive the federal subminimum wage of $2.13 per hour, restaurant workers in nineteen other states receive a subminimum wage that is $5 per hour or less, and another eight states have a subminimum wage that is higher than $5 an hour. Tipped workers in only seven states—Alaska, California, Minnesota, Montana, Nevada, Oregon, and Washington—receive the full minimum wage because those states have chosen to pay an equal wage to both tipped and non-tipped workers. Despite the rhetoric of the other NRA insisting that paying a full minimum wage would kill the restaurant industry and reduce workers' tips, these seven states have the same or higher restaurant establishment growth rates, the same or higher tipped worker job growth rates, and the same or higher tipping averages.

When people think of tipped workers, they think of workers clearing tables, taking orders, or running food out for restaurant patrons, or bartenders. It's true that the restaurant industry continues to be the largest segment of tipped workers. (The restaurant industry is actually one of the largest employers in the United States altogether; with over thirteen million workers in the industry, prior to the pandemic nearly one in ten American workers currently works in restaurants, and one in two Americans has worked in the industry at some point in their lifetime.) But there are tipped workers in all sectors of the service industry. Tipped workers carry our luggage, they wash or park our cars, they do our mani-pedis, they give us massages, they cut and style our hair, they deliver our food and groceries for DoorDash or Instacart, and they drive us to work and play for Uber or Lyft. Workers who enter into tipped occupations do so because these jobs provide them an opportunity to work and quickly begin earning ready cash to support their families. Tipped workers put themselves at our service, tolerating abusive employers and, at times, customers, navigating unstable tipped wages that vary by shift and season. Their dependence on tips, which fluctuate wildly, makes them vulnerable to sexual and other forms of harassment, and even assault.

There are now roughly six million workers who are paid the subminimum wage and depend on tips to make ends meet. The National Restaurant Association may have initiated the idea of a subminimum wage for tipped workers, but now the idea of tips as a replacement for wages has spread across the economy. The existence of a subminimum wage continues to create an incentive for more sectors to follow the restaurant industry in a race to the bottom, and that means the number of workers who are forced to live off the whims and fancies of customers to feed their families only grows. Increasingly, these workers are the backbone of the gig economy. Workers who are misclassified as independent contractors—so that their employers can avoid paying them wages and benefits—provide taxi services, deliver foods and goods, and take care of your household chores, all at the touch of an app, increasingly depend on tips to augment meager base pay—a subminimum wage.[12]

The persistence of subminimum pay is a direct reflection of who tipped workers are. Today, two-thirds of tipped workers in the United States are women who work in casual restaurants, nail salons, hair salons, and many other environments where tips are meager. They struggle with three times the poverty rate of the rest of the U.S. workforce and who use food stamps at double the rate. Black tipped workers were always majority women.

Moreover, starting in the 1980s, the service sector experienced rapid demographic change, with immigrant workers transforming the industry. The Immigration Reform and Control Act of the 1960s had allowed an initial wave of Black and brown immigrants into the United States; by the 1980s they were being followed by family members, by refugees of the Cold War from Latin America and Asia, and by refugees from the World Bank's austerity policies in the global South. Foreign-born workers made up 10 percent of the restaurant workforce in 1980; this number grew to 25 percent by 2010. Nearly one out of four workers in the restaurant industry is now foreign-born,[13] and tipped restaurant workers who were foreign-born grew from 9 percent to 19 percent in that same period.[14] Estimates from the Pew Hispanic Center suggest that up to half of these workers are undocumented.[15]

Immigrant tipped workers can be found in every state of the nation, and they come from all over the world. While it is true that half of all immigrant workers come from Latin America, there are sizable populations of workers from Asia, Africa, and Europe that vary by occupation. Workers from Asia, for example, are a majority of nail salon and gaming service workers and most massage therapists. Workers from Africa are concentrated among taxi drivers, valet workers, and bellhops. Immigrants from Europe, meanwhile, are overrepresented among massage therapists, bartenders, and hosts. Workers from Latin America are heavily concentrated among car wash workers, bussers, and runners, while also being a majority of immigrant bartenders, counter attendants, servers, delivery workers, hosts, barbers, and valets.

In New York and Washington, DC, tipped workers are also mostly immigrants and people of color. In DC, tipped workers are slightly more than half foreign-born and more than two-thirds people of color. Immigrants comprise nearly half of all tipped workers in New York State, and almost two-thirds of tipped workers in New York City.

As tipped workers, they are subject to incredibly unstable livelihoods; and as mostly women, they are vulnerable to sexual harassment and even assault. Their experiences of economic insecurity, customer harassment, and exploitation by employers are shared by a wide majority of service workers nationally, including white men. Their experiences are increasingly the experiences of all workers.

What's more, tipped workers include not only millions who are undocumented but also millions more who are documented—studying or working on a visa, living as a permanent resident on a green card, or even naturalized citizens. In today's America some face a triple vulnerability—as immigrants and people of color, they live in constant insecurity as to their future in the country.

Other Subminimum Wage Workers

Unfortunately, tipped workers are not alone in earning a subminimum wage that is a direct legacy of slavery.

The Thirteenth Amendment, which ended slavery, allows for an exception to the abolishment of slavery and involuntary servitude, "as punishment for crime whereof the party shall have been duly convicted." When Southern states lost their access to free labor, they turned to criminalization of Black people in order to recoup their losses. Southern states established "convict leasing" programs, to lease prisoners to private individuals and corporations who often perpetrated torture and abuse on these workers even as they exploited their labor. In some cases, these workers were worked to death; in 2018, a mass grave with the remains of ninety-five African American forced laborers were found in Texas that research shown had been worked to death.[16] Political pressure to end the torturous convict leasing system resulted in modified programs such as chain gangs and prison farms—continued extensions of slavery that persist to this day.[17]

Today, based on this same exception to the Thirteenth Amendment, nine hundred thousand incarcerated workers in multiple states continue to be paid no wage for their labor, and this free or very low-cost labor continues to be exploited by private industry.[18] Unfortunately, the Prison Policy Initiative reports that the average wage for prisoners has actually gone down in the last several years as several Southern states have reduced their maximum wages for prisoners. Wages differ based on whether workers are employed by the prison itself or by an outside corporation. The PPI reports that the average minimum daily wage paid to incarcerated workers for nonindustry prison jobs is 86 cents, but that public sector prison jobs go completely unpaid in Alabama, Arkansas, Florida, Georgia, and Texas.[19] About 6 percent of incarcerated people may work for state-owned businesses and earn between 33 cents and $1.41 per hour on average, and an even smaller percentage work for private companies like Victoria's Secret, Whole Foods, Nintendo, and Eddie Bauer, along with many others that have processing facilities inside prisons and pay similar subminimum wages. These companies hired incarcerated people through the federal government's Prison Industry Enhancement Certification Program (PIECP)—a means for private industry to continue to obtain nearly free labor.[20] In 2015, Whole Foods was exposed and criticized for paying prisoners as little as

74 cents a day to construct fish tanks and raise tilapia that is then sold for $11.99 a pound at Whole Foods.[21] In 2016 and 2018, incarcerated people staged nationwide strikes to fight their paltry wages and literal slave labor.[22]

Most states deduct a wide variety of expenses from prisoners' meager paychecks for discharge costs, court fees, victim funds, and more, limiting prisoners' ability to pay for basic hygiene products that are often not available in the prison. Some states argue that these work programs provide training for prisoners when they leave, but data shows that for the most part formerly incarcerated workers struggle to find work that allows them to use any skills or experience they gained while inside, leading to high rates of recidivism when they are not able to find work to support themselves or their families.[23]

The subminimum wage reflects a devaluation of work and stems from a history of exclusion and exploitation. Like tipped workers, people with disabilities were excluded from the Fair Labor Standards Act, the nation's first minimum wage law passed in 1938 as part of the New Deal. Section 14(c) provision of the Fair Labor Standards Act permits employers who are certified by the U.S. Department of Labor to pay disabled employees at rates that are lower than the minimum wage set by Congress.[24] The rates vary by state and even by employer.

Congress has allowed workers with disabilities to be isolated in "sheltered workshops," based on the antiquated notion that people with disabilities had to be segregated from others because doctors and other practitioners did not know how else to care for them, based on the assumption that they could not care for themselves.[25] Ninety-five percent of workers with disabilities earning the subminimum wage work in sheltered workshops. According to the Center for American Progress, "The intent of the 14(c) provision was to encourage the hiring of people with disabilities and facilitate their transition to fully integrated work settings where they are paid wages at competitive rates commensurate with their nondisabled peers. However, this purported goal is predicated on the presumption that disabled workers' labor is less valuable and therefore warrants what is fundamentally a separate and unequal pay structure."[26]

During the civil rights era, advocates began pushing back against this paternalistic, custodial attitude, which led to a series of laws mandating equal access and equal treatment for Americans with disabilities. The landmark Americans with Disabilities Act of 1990 made it illegal for the first time for employers to discriminate against workers who had disabilities. However, the ADA didn't address the 1938 federal law that allows businesses to pay less than minimum wage in some cases. Since 2015, New Hampshire, Maryland, and then Alaska all banned subminimum wages for people with disabilities, and many more states have introduced legislation to follow suit.

Following arguments similar to those that support subminimum wages for Americans with disabilities, many states have set subminimum wages for teenage workers, in response to lobbying from corporate trade associations. These groups have argued that employers will be forced to reduce teen employment if they pay young people a full minimum wage. However, numerous studies have shown that teenagers today are supporting their families—in some cases they are sole or primary breadwinners—and that raising the minimum wage does not affect teen employment.[27]

Each chapter of this book tells the story of one or more tipped workers in one of seven tipped occupations, and highlights the key issues tipped workers in that occupation face. All of these workers have precarious lives, and in the case of immigrant workers, these are exacerbated by additional challenges that are both a symptom of this precariousness and add to it.

Trupti is an Indian-Ugandan-American server in DC who has faced constant sexual harassment in the various restaurants in which she has worked; restaurant servers are mostly women, who face the highest rates of sexual harassment of any occupation. Teto was a busser from Mexico living in Arizona who was never allowed to move up into a server position given his skin color and the racial segregation of the restaurant industry. Vianne is a tech platform delivery worker, also from Mexico, who has worked in several different tech platform delivery companies and has experienced the high levels of stress that delivery workers face today—impacting her health. Angel is an Uber driver from Puerto Rico who has been driven to overwork, a common experience of Uber and Lyft drivers who are deceptively drawn into working endless hours by a platform that lacks transparency with regard to hours, pay, and tips. For Yenelia, a nail salon worker from Honduras living in New York, the uncertainty of tip income combined with the uncertainty of life as an immigrant is exacerbated by the health risks of the chemicals that nail technicians are exposed to all day long. Dia and Adrinne are African American parking lot and wheelchair attendants in Washington, DC, and Houston, TX, respectively, who struggle to make ends meet on tips from wealthy customers who have them park their cars. Debbie and Marshan tell the stories of working for subminimum pay while incarcerated, Frances shares the experience of working for the subminimum wage for workers with disabilities, and Fiona shares the victory that she and other youth workers won in New Jersey to end subminimum wages for youth workers.

This book is based on the findings of over five hundred interviews with restaurant and other tipped and subminimum wage workers, over ten thousand surveys of restaurant workers, and government data analysis. Both the surveys and interviews included thousands of workers. In order to bring the experience of many different subminimum wage workers to life, we also conducted more in-depth interviews with over two dozen subminimum wage workers in several different sectors coming from multiple cities around the country. Through our surveys and interviews we have learned of the experiences and struggles that these workers face on a daily basis, and that many have faced for decades.

We hope their stories will highlight the struggles of millions of workers like them—and the real possibilities for a better world.

2

Trupti

Serving with Sexual Harassment

"Take off your mask so I know how much to tip you"

Trupti Patel was born in Zambia, where her Indian parents had lived for five years working in the medical profession before coming to the United States.

Trupti's mother and father had met at Baroda Medical College in the state of Gujarat, India; she was in nursing school and he was in medical school. Upon graduation and their marriage, Trupti's mother started working as a nurse and her father was recruited by the United Nations Development Programme to practice medicine in a nearby rural village. The UN noted Trupti's father's work and recruited him into the World Health Organization, inviting him to practice medicine in Zambia. Trupti's mother followed him to Zambia and was able to continue her nursing work there. A few years later, Trupti was born. "My family had a really good life in Africa; they were really happy."

However, when Trupti was six months old, political strife in Uganda forced her family to leave. The couple and their

newborn baby immigrated to the United States in the early 1980s, and eventually moved to Louisiana.

In America, Trupti faced unfamiliar discrimination. "I was the only brown kid at school; no one looked like me. They made fun of me for having a different name, different food." Trupti's vegetarian parents told her to eat meat—or whatever the school cafeteria served—to fit in. Trupti's many experiences of discrimination in Louisiana left a lasting impression. "It shaped my perception of immigrant rights and social justice issues. I noticed that if you didn't speak like them, sound like them, you were automatically told that the only position you could have would be to be in service to someone else. You could never be a professional."

Trupti noted that these attitudes extended not just to
herself but also to a small local Vietnamese community,
and to the African American community, though percep-
tions of these groups seemed to shift, always at the whims
of the white population. "The Black community was also
seen as inferior, but sometimes immigrants would be seen
as beneath the Black community, sometimes they'd be seen
as above. It would depend. But the general consensus was
that white people looked at communities of color as being
beneath them—that they should be in positions of service
or servitude. You looked at people with office jobs—they
were white women. Women of color were custodians. Fast-
food workers were African American women and men. All
immigrants were told 'I can't understand what you're saying,' even when they were strong English speakers. If they
had an accent they'd be told 'You can't speak English.' My
parents were articulate English speakers, but because of their
accent, they were told they couldn't be understood. White
people in the South had strong Southern accents, 'but that
accent was seen as more appealing.'"

Trupti stayed local for college, but after graduation she
was accepted into George Washington University's School
of Political Management master's degree program. She ended up working on Capitol Hill until the 2008 election. She
wanted to work on the Obama campaign, and left her job
to do so—only to find that the campaigns had frozen hiring in the midst of the Democratic Party nomination battle

between Obama and Hillary Clinton. Trupti ended up taking work as a lobbyist in the meantime, and was laid off when the recession hit.

At that point, Trupti was ready to take any job. She worked multiple short-term jobs—as an administrative assistant, at Trader Joe's—until a friend who was a bartender invited her to apply at the Indian restaurant where she worked. Trupti was hired almost instantly as a host, and fell into the restaurant industry professionally.

Trupti started as a host but moved up quickly to be a bartender in the Indian restaurant because she spoke better English than most of the immigrant workers. "I immediately saw the injustices of the hospitality industry. The patrons treated me differently from the servers because I spoke English with no accent. The patrons would treat me better, call me over to say what they wanted, rather than telling the server. They'd say, 'We prefer to talk to you than the server.' I'd notice the immigrant servers and bussers being mistreated a lot more by management because English wasn't their first language. They'd tell the immigrant workers, 'You're lucky to have this job. Who would hire you? You're an immigrant.' I noticed the meanness, and it reminded me of how my parents were treated. I didn't like it when people were picked on. It was a method of control, because a lot of staff were undocumented. They'd say, 'Don't try to think about finding another job, because you have no papers. Who's gonna hire you?'"

When she talked to the immigrant workers, Trupti found they were willing to put up with the abuse in order to have something to eat. "They were people who didn't have any other options. I was always known as the nice one, explaining to people their rights, telling them 'They're not gonna call immigration on you. You don't have to tell your status.' They would ask me to help them fill stuff out. I always looked at immigrant workers in the way my parents were treated. My parents at least could read and speak English, but they still suffered, in some cases worse. I noticed a trend—management always seemed harsher toward immigrant workers. In one restaurant, immigrant workers weren't told how they'd be paid. They were just given pay and told 'This is what your pay is.' They'd make sure immigrant workers were always bussers, never speaking to patrons."

Trupti took pride in her work and stayed in the industry, but struggled herself with wages and working conditions. "The customers really liked me; I had fun. I enjoyed it. But I learned quickly about economic anxiety, living off tips. The owners really didn't mess with me the way they messed with others—because they knew I knew my rights and English was my first language. I was privileged, I had rights, they couldn't afford to bully me as much." Even then, Trupti still faced harassment and abuse.

"I walked out of the [Indian] restaurant when the owner started screaming at me," she recalled. "He said, 'I'm not going to pay you.' So I went to the Department of Employment Services, and got my money back within twenty-four hours."

In addition to multiple instances of wage theft, Trupti also experienced sexual harassment. "At the Indian restaurant, a chef in the back of the house liked to make sexual comments. If you didn't flirt back, the food would come out late, come out cold, come out wrong. If you rebuffed the advances, he'd use anger to get back at you. We let the manager know that he screwed up the food, and the chef would come up with excuses like 'They put the order in wrong.' The manager would tell the chef not to talk to us like that, and it would stop for a while, but then it would start right over again."

In this instance, the chef had the power to impact Trupti's tips based on her willingness to flirt with him, based on how he produced the meals. And of course customers had even more direct power to impact Trupti's tips based on how willing she was to flirt. "I had a group of male customers in a Mexican restaurant where I worked. The man in the party was tipsy, handsy, kept putting his hands on me, grabbing my arm, other parts of my body. I had to keep telling him to stop touching me. A lot of male patrons are essentially saying to me, 'Flirt with me—you need to entertain me to get the tip.' A couple months ago I was bartending and there was a guy who sat at my bar. You have to chat them up to get more tips. The guy was from out of town. . . . After a couple of minutes he asked, 'So, what's there to do in town?' I told him where he should go—what clubs, what bars. He said, 'Can you come with me later?' and winked at me. Now at that point—if you say no, he will get pissed and leave no tip. Or if you say 'I'll come with you,' so that he'll leave the tip, then he might stalk you. So instead I said, 'Let me see when I get out of here.' I always give myself some space, make up some lie. I'll say, 'Maybe my friend and I will stop by.' There are always those incidents where they feel like they have power over you because of the tip."

Trupti noticed that other women also felt they must encourage the harassment to get tips. "One of my female colleagues . . . came in, and her shirt was unbuttoned so you could see her cleavage. I said, 'Hey, you might want to button that up.' I thought maybe she didn't realize. She said, 'Oh honey that's how I'm working the tip today.' Even management doesn't tell you to do it, you're gonna act and portray yourself in a manner that feeds this environment. I know there's a thin line between being hospitable and play-ful and sexual harassment. But it's encouraging women to continue this cycle. My female colleague may not feel like it's a big deal, but I won't do it—I should be tipped based on my service." Trupti notes that as a result of this cycle, women who are "skinnier, bustier" are given higher-tipping sections and shifts.

Over the last six years of leading the campaign for One Fair Wage, we have consistently run into the misperception that the prototypical tipped worker is a fine dining server who earns a great deal of money in tips. This misperception is driven by the personal experiences of some of the key audiences we are trying to educate. Quite often these professionals tend to frequent fine dining establishments, taking colleagues or business meetings to upscale dining environments. Or they recall earning substantial income in tips as fine dining or upscale servers in their youth, during their college or graduate school days. So their perception of who tipped workers are is entirely based on this narrow experience of a sliver of the tipped worker economy.

Restaurant servers are 75 percent of all tipped workers, but the vast majority of restaurant servers do not work in fine dining environments. Our research shows that less than one-third of all restaurant servers work in fine dining environments, and this proportion is far less for immigrant servers and servers of color, who very rarely are hired as fine dining servers. The majority of all restaurant servers work in casual restaurants, including "family-style" chain restaurants like IHOP, Denny's, Applebee's, Olive Garden, and the like, but also in diners, taverns and bars, and small casual restaurants focused on the cuisine of a particular nationality; Mexican, Chinese, Indian, and Thai being among the most popular cuisines for this particular type of casual restaurant.

Almost all immigrant servers work in these many different types of casual restaurants. And while the majority of restaurant servers who work in casual restaurants face a myriad of challenges including severe economic instability, vulnerability to sexual and other forms of harassment, and stress and health issues, for immigrant servers all of these issues are greatly exacerbated. Nearly one in five servers in America is an immigrant.

Tipped workers occupy a uniquely vulnerable position in our nation's employment landscape. Poverty rates for tipped workers—particularly for women, who make up 66 percent of all tipped workers, and for people of color, who make up 40 percent of the total—are higher in states that pay a $2.13 subminimum wage than in states that pay one minimum wage for tipped and non-tipped workers. As a result, tipped restaurant workers are expected to collect the remainder of their wages from customers' tips, creating an environment in which a majority female workforce must please and curry favor with customers to earn a living.

Two-thirds of all restaurant servers nationwide are women, and 40 percent are single mothers. The economic position of all women restaurant workers is precarious; the situation of immigrant women servers even more so.[1] Women restaurant workers experience poverty at nearly one and one-third the rate of men restaurant workers.[2] Women's greater economic insecurity in the industry is largely attributable to their greater likelihood of being employed as tipped workers. While women are 52 percent of all restaurant employees, they are two-thirds or 66 percent of all tipped restaurant workers.[3] A majority of these tipped workers are employed in casual, family-style restaurants where tips are meager. The median wage for tipped workers hovers around $9 an hour including tips.[4]

Restaurant servers suffer among the highest rates of sexual harassment of any industry—our research shows that 90 percent of both men and women servers report experiencing sexual harassment on a regular basis—and this is largely due to the fluctuating nature of their incomes. Given the fact that the subminimum wage for tipped workers forces restaurant servers to earn the majority of their income in tips, women servers must tolerate inappropriate customer behavior to feed their families almost exclusively in tips. Beyond tolerance of such behavior, however, managers actually encourage women to dress provocatively and flirt with customers in order to make more money in tips—subjecting themselves to objectification not only from customers but also from coworkers and management.[5]

This dynamic contributes to the restaurant industry's status as the single largest source of sexual harassment claims in the United States. While 7 percent of American women work in the restaurant industry, more than one-third (an eye-opening 37 percent) of all sexual harassment claims to the Equal Employment Opportunity Commission (EEOC) come from the restaurant industry.[6] Even these high levels of complaints to the EEOC may underreport the industry's rate of sexual harassment. Restaurant workers in focus groups we conducted in our national study on sexual harassment in the restaurant industry noted that sexual harassment is "kitchen talk," a "normalized" part of the work environment and that many restaurant workers, particularly immigrant workers, are reluctant to publicly acknowledge their experiences with sexual harassment.[7]

In 2014 we released a report called "The Glass Floor" referring to the system that leaves women and all workers in a state of insecurity because of the intersection of economic precariousness and a sexualized work atmosphere. To examine the incidence of unwanted sexual behavior and sexual harassment in the restaurant industry, the organization I co-founded and led, ROC United, and a sister organization called Forward Together surveyed 688 current and former restaurant workers across 39 states. The study found that sexual harassment in restaurants is widespread and is experienced by all types of workers. The highly sexualized environment in which restaurant workers labor impacts every major workplace relationship, with restaurant workers reporting high levels of harassing behaviors from restaurant management (66 percent), coworkers (80 percent), and customers (78 percent).

One of the most powerful findings of "The Glass Floor" is the extent to which the industry's already high levels of sex harassment are exacerbated by systems in which tipped restaurant workers—primarily women—endure legalized pay discrimination in the form of a subminimum wage. In states that allow a subminimum wage for tipped workers, these workers' hourly wages are so low that they often go entirely to taxes, forcing millions of tipped restaurant workers, the vast majority of whom are women, to live entirely off their tips. Living off tips makes an industry already rife with sexual harassment even more dangerous. Women restaurant workers living off tips in states where the subminimum wage for tipped workers is $2.13 per hour are twice as likely to experience sexual harassment as women in states that pay the same minimum wage to all workers.[8] Tipped women workers in $2.13 states reported that they were three times more likely to be told by management to alter their appearance and to wear "sexier," more revealing clothing than they were in states where the same minimum wage was paid to all workers. Conversely, tipped women workers in states that have eliminated the subminimum wage were less likely to experience sexual harassment. As it turns out, when women are paid a full minimum wage, and tips are an extra or bonus as they were always intended to be, they do not feel as much of need to tolerate or encourage customer harassment as women in states in which tips are the bulk of their wage.

Importantly, subminimum wages impact all workers in the industry—not just tipped workers. All workers in states with a $2.13 subminimum wage, including men and non-tipped workers, reported higher rates of sexual harassment, indicating that the overall restaurant work environment is at least partially shaped by the subminimum wage system itself.

These findings were confirmed in a March 2021 study One Fair Wage conducted in partnership with Professor Catharine MacKinnon, the world-renowned legal scholar who coined the term "sexual harassment" and then successfully fought over decades to make it illegal. Together with Professor MacKinnon we published the report "The Tipping Point: How the Subminimum Wage Keeps Incomes Low and Harassment High," based on the nation's first nationally representative study of restaurant workers' experiences with sexual harassment. The study provided irrefutable evidence that relying on tips is what Professor MacKinnon calls "the motherlode" of sexual harassment—higher than all other sectors studied, she said, including the military. The study found that 71 percent of tipped workers reported experiencing sexual harassment, compared to 56 percent of non-tipped workers, and that they also faced much higher retaliation for complaining about harassment than their non-tipped counterparts—indicating the level of expectation by management that harassment is to be normalized and accepted by tipped workers.[9]

All of these findings became grossly exacerbated during the pandemic. In our fall 2020 survey of nearly two thousand service workers, more than 40 percent reported that sexual harassment had increased during the pandemic. Hundreds of women submitted comments they had received from male customers asking them to remove their masks in order to judge their looks and thus their tips on that basis.

Since these workers were also being asked to serve as health marshals—enforcing social distancing and mask rules in one of the most dangerous environments of all—they became "essential workers." Tipped service workers thus became one of the only essential workers to not receive a full minimum wage, and the only essential workers to be asked to remove their protective gear for a chance to earn their income. The research obliterated the idea that tipping is based solely on the quality of service received, and not biased based on the server's race, gender, appearance, and willingness to tolerate objectification and harassment. It also emphasized the need to ensure these workers receive a full minimum wage so that they do not feel compelled to remove their masks, potentially exposing both themselves and everyone else in the restaurant to the pandemic.

The high levels of sexual harassment experienced by all restaurant workers—and by women and tipped restaurant workers in particular—are even more troubling given that the size of the industry means that many young women in America are introduced to the world of work in a restaurant. A restaurant job is often the first job a young woman obtains, whether she stays in the industry her whole life or moves on to another career.[10] This environment is where many women first learn their worth as workers. Countless young women start out as early as high school working as part-time servers, bussers, hostesses, and dishwashers in casual, family restaurants and fast-food chains that are notorious for low wages, poor sanitary and safety conditions, and sexual harassment. A negative first experience in the restaurant increases the likelihood that women will come to expect sexual harassment in other work environments. In our study, women who had previously worked as tipped workers were 1.6 times as likely to live with harassing behaviors in the workplace as the women who were currently employed as tipped workers.

It is critical to contextualize the concept of "living with" sexual harassment in the workplace as something different than consent. Our survey and focus group results show that most workers either ignore or put up with harassing behaviors because they fear they will be penalized through loss of income from tips, unfavorable shifts, public humiliation, or even job loss. At the same time, workers are taking steps to address the impact of harassment on their well-being. Seventy-six percent of workers who experienced sexual harassment talked to their families and friends about their experiences, 73 percent talked to their coworkers, and 44 percent talked to a supervisor. Eighty-eight percent of workers who experienced sexual harassment reported that they'd be more likely to talk to their supervisor about these experiences if they were part of a group of coworkers.

Together these findings paint a troubling portrait of endemic sexual harassment in the restaurant industry. Widespread harassment, particularly toward women and tipped workers, demonstrates how power is used to exert control over other workers' bodies and livelihoods. Our data shows that all too often the economic insecurity of living off tips contributes to higher levels of physical insecurity being reported by all restaurant workers—and particularly women and women of color restaurant workers—in a workplace rife with sexual harassment. In order to reduce the pressures that increase sexual harassment, we must eliminate the subminimum wage for tipped workers while implementing and strengthening policies to educate workers on their rights and reduce rates of sexual harassment. Legislating One Fair Wage, so all workers are ensured a minimum wage sufficient to cover their basic needs, and eliminating a subminimum wage for tipped workers, can give all workers greater personal agency, creating a safer and more equitable workplace.

Since one in two Americans works in restaurants at some point in their lifetime, and since for most of these Americans, restaurants are their first job, these early experiences of sexual harassment have lifelong impacts. Through the process of surveying and interviewing restaurant workers for the "Glass Floor" study, women recounted being told by their managers to "dress more sexy, show more cleavage, and wear tighter clothing" in order to earn more money in tips. In this way, young women are not told to tolerate sexual harassment—they are encouraged to encourage it. And as the first job for so many young women, the restaurant trains young women in what is considered acceptable, normal, legal, and ethical in the workplace. We repeatedly heard from older women that they had experienced sexual harassment later in life, in their current professions, but did nothing about it because "it was never as bad as it was when I was a young woman working in restaurants." In this way, because of the subminimum wage and its direct link to sexual harassment, not only does the restaurant industry have the highest rates of sexual harassment of any industry—it also sets the standard for what is considered acceptable for women across the economy.

For most young women in their first job, the power dynamics between these women and their managers, coworkers, and customers are extreme, since they have no ability to compare their first experience on the job to any other experience, or to push back on the basis of an understanding that what they are experiencing is wrong or illegal.

In May 2019, Representative Alexandria Ocasio-Cortez agreed to conduct a "Server for an Hour" event with the One Fair Wage campaign to elevate the need to legislate a full, fair minimum wage for tipped workers with tips on top. At the event, Representative Ocasio-Cortez, who has called for a more just immigration system, artfully described the connection between the subminimum wage and harassment. "Maybe you can ignore the harassing customer if it's the first or the fifteenth of the month. But by the twenty-ninth or thirtieth, you're going to put up with that guy who asks for your number or touches you in a certain way, because you rely on those tips to pay the rent."

A few years ago, Trupti became a leader in the fight for One Fair Wage. Based on her experiences of economic instability and sexual harassment living off the subminimum wage for tipped workers, she helped to lead the fight to put One Fair Wage on the ballot in Washington, DC, which then became known as Initiative 77. During this intensely fought campaign, restaurant owners across the city told their staff members that their tips would disappear with Initiative 77, and instructed them to wear buttons saying "No on 77" and to tell patrons to vote against the measure because they would lose their tips. Workers felt compelled to do this for fear of retaliation, which was real.

Trupti experienced it herself. The restaurant where she worked during the campaign, in which she was a vocal public face, reduced her hours from full-time to just one shift. "They had a manager that they put to punish me. . . . They appointed him to be the bully and the harasser." Trupti reported that he would scream at her and belittle her in an attempt to push her out. "When being mean didn't work, he started acting inappropriately. I was working behind the bar, and he came up behind me and placed a kiss on back of my neck. I wanted to throw up. I think he was trying to figure out what would make me most uncomfortable. He was bipolar. One minute he'd be a raging maniac, screaming 'You're incompetent!' At other times, he'd put his arms around me [and] say 'You've worked so hard for me,' and kiss me on my check. I didn't complain—I had already been so worn down from constant harassment and bullying that he put me through." Trupti hinted about her discomfort to another manager, who witnessed some of the harassment, but the other manager said nothing and did nothing.

Trupti feels this kind of abuse is worse for immigrant women and women of color. "They're the ones who will bury it, put up with it, because they feel the vulnerability of being an immigrant. They're realizing that this is their income they're using to feed their families. It's harder when they're new immigrants, they feel even though there are rights, it doesn't apply to them, because they're so new. They'll say 'I have rights, but where am I going to work, my priority is that I have to feed my kids.'" Trupti notes a woman of color who tolerates the screaming bartender, for example. "She's a single mom raising two kids. She and the hostile male bartender got into it yesterday. She says, 'I have to keep my mouth shut, because I can't let this guy cost me my job, I have to put food on the table.'"

For Trupti's part, she helped lead Initiative 77 to victory. After the victory, when the DC City Council was heavily lobbied and bribed by the National Restaurant Association to overturn the will of the people, Trupti's experiences as a restaurant worker moved her to run for elected office herself. She became a DC neighborhood commissioner, vowing to stand up for DC's immigrant workers, who are actually the majority of tipped workers in the District. She worked hard to successfully help elect candidates to the DC City Council who supported reinstating Initiative 77 in the November 2020 election, and is now working to make sure the DC Council actually does so. "I'm always going to stand up for hospitality industry rights," Trupti says.

3

Teto

Jim Crow Segregation for Tipped Workers

"Once a busser, forever a busser"

Teto was born in Agua Prieta in the state of Sonora, Mexico, when his father was eighteen and his mother seventeen. His father had been working as a factory supervisor in his future father-in-law's company when they met, married, and had Teto. Teto's father quit his job and the young couple started a restaurant, serving grilled chicken and *carne asada*. The business thrived for a while, until one spring day the restaurant workers failed to show up and Teto's father was forced to close the restaurant.

Teto's parents struggled for a whole year to find another job. "There were basically three options for men to find work in Mexico at that time," said Teto. "You had a business, you were 'in the business' [organized crime], or you worked as a factory worker." His father's friends were "in the business," and his mother worried about his father getting involved: it was too dangerous, not to mention inappropriate, for a new husband and father. When Teto was four, relatives in Tucson invited the young family to try a new life across the border, and the family accepted. Tucson was just two hours away.

Tucson is a border town. At the time, in the mid-nineties, crossing the border was as simple as signing a form. "The border towns rely on one another," Teto said. "People cross the border multiple times a day to go to Walmart or to work. It wasn't that big of a trip for my family to drive two hours to try something new in Tucson." The family had tourist visas like everyone else crossing the border, but neither his parents—nor he, when he became old enough—had permission to work.

As a four-year-old arriving in the United States, Teto was in awe of his new surroundings. "I actually remember very vividly the day that we came. I remember the first time being in Tucson, just the difference in the culture." Teto ended up attending a bilingual school, which helped him solidify his English and Spanish. "It was a really, really good school. I feel like I was very immersed in both cultures. . . . I had a speech impediment, a lisp. And the school had classes for it. They actually helped me get rid of my lisp."

After a few years, Teto's family had the opportunity to move from the south side of Tucson to the north, a more affluent part of town where the schools were better. "My school was named an A+ Arizona school fifteen times; it had a lot to offer. We had dance, fine arts, and theater, and I was very involved." Teto embraced school, secure in a stable childhood growing up in Tucson. "I lived a very normal

American life. I graduated top of my class in high school with a 4.0."

Although he had been brought to the United States at the age of four, Teto knew that there were no real immediate options for him to obtain legal residency or citizenship in the United States. "I didn't qualify for DACA (Deferred Action for Childhood Arrivals)." People suggested he wait until his sister turned twenty-one or until other members of his family were able to sponsor him. He despaired. "It would be over ten years."

The first experience Teto had working in a restaurant was as a busser at the Mexican sports bar-restaurant in Tucson where his mother worked. He was thirteen and still in school. "I started as a bus[ser] and I would bus during the summer," he said. "I started and I would bus five days a week and then, when I started school up again, I stayed working during the weekends."

As a busser, Teto's hands were full. He would greet customers, take them to their seats, bring them drinks, run food to the tables, clean tables, sweep floors, clean windows, and take out the trash. "I'd also pick up the slack for servers," he said. "Sometimes the servers would let me take a few tables—take the orders." Teto worked as a busser in the restaurant for eight years, until he was twenty-one, and throughout that period he was always asking to be promoted to server. He would tell the manager, "I feel like I have the

personality. When I do take tables [as a server], the customers love me. But the manager would always make the same
excuse. 'You're good at your job. You're the best busboy we
have.'"

While the owners of the restaurant were Mexican, the
manager was a light-skinned, blond Mexican man who preferred a certain "look" for the servers. All the servers were
white women and all the bussers were Latino men. The
bussers took home approximately $500 per week, and serv-
ers would take home closer to $1,000 per week. And there
was no chance of Teto getting a promotion. "The white
girls would get promoted right away to be a server, and we'd
be stuck as bussers. But I knew everything better than the
servers. Whenever there was a new worker, they'd get sent
to me to get trained. I knew the menu better, the customers better, I knew the restaurant better, but I never got the
chance to be a server."

Teto directly confronted the manager and asked if it was
because he wasn't a blond female. The manager always
denied this, but everyone could see through his excuse,
and Teto's resentment grew. "There were lots of tensions
between the bussers and the servers, between the bussers
and management." At the age of twenty-one, after eight
years of waiting to become a server, Teto finally quit. "I
told them I was sick of waiting to be a server, and that I was
moving on to find a better opportunity."

The position of busser has a long racial history in the

United States. The great poet Langston Hughes worked as
a busser (or busboy to use the terminology of the day, when
all Black men were referred to as "boy") in a restaurant in
a Washington, DC, hotel. In his autobiography, Hughes
recounts struggling to find the few jobs allowed to African
Americans in 1920s America.[1] He found work as a sailor
loading, transporting, and unloading merchandise for ship-
ping companies, and then worked in Europe as a dishwasher
in a restaurant in Paris. On his return to the United States,
Hughes ended up in the capital, a place he found more segregated than any that he had lived in previously. There were
few opportunities to find work, and he often went without
food and proper clothing. One of the few positions open to
Black workers at the time was working as a busboy, and it
was while working as a busser at a hotel that he read in the
paper that the famed poet Vachel Lindsay would be visiting
the area. Hughes felt he could not speak directly to Lindsay,
but left three of his own poems beside Lindsay's plate. The
next morning, the newspapers announced that Lindsay had
"discovered" an African American busser poet, and report-
ers swarmed the restaurant to take Hughes's picture. It was
this incident that catapulted Hughes to national fame.

Of course, most bussers are never "discovered." An inte-
gral part of the busser's role is to remain invisible as he or she
cleans the table and sets it for the next guest, takes dishes and
silverware to be cleaned in the kitchen, brings bread to the
table, refills water glasses, and helps the servers with table

service. A busser may also be asked to clean furniture, the floors, and anything else that might need cleaning. Guides on busser etiquette emphasize that bussers should not speak to or interact with guests. Because it is an invisible position, it has been occupied by men and sometimes women of color in large metropolitan areas of the United States for over a century—first African Americans, and now immigrants of color. The title may have changed from busboy to busser, but the invisibility and lack of mobility have not.

Prior to the pandemic, the restaurant industry employed over 13.6 million workers nationwide, providing not only the largest source of minimum-wage jobs but also high-earning professional careers. Almost 80 percent of the industry earns low and poverty wages, while the remaining 20 percent who earn a living wage are mostly servers and bartenders in fine dining restaurants.[2] The industry's growth is resilient. As the industry reopens and the pandemic declines, as one of the largest and fastest-growing industries with an expanding slew of positions, restaurants could offer a sustainable career ladder to thousands of people living in an increasingly precarious economy; they could provide real pathways to living wage professions for Black, Latinx, Asian, and Indigenous workers. Yet the truth is that many of the industry's best-paying jobs are still not available to everyone.

Workers of color comprise almost half of the restaurant workforce nationwide and the majority of the workforce in states like New York and California, but the current structure of the industry denies living wage opportunities to a large percentage of this diverse workforce, and the subminimum wage for tipped workers exacerbates the racial income gap created by the segregation. Around 30 percent of bussers are immigrants, but that percentage goes down to 20 percent among servers, and 10 percent among bartenders.[3] Immigrants and other workers of color are segregated into lower-paying positions—like bussers—and lower-paying segments of the industry, like fast food and casual restaurants. In the forty-three states with a subminimum wage, tips are a larger percentage of workers' base pay, and the fact that immigrants and people of color are relegated into lower-paying positions and into lower-paying casual restaurants results in even greater poverty rates, instability, and precariousness for them. The subminimum wage for tipped workers exacerbates the racial segregation for two reasons: first, tipped workers of color are relegated to lower-tipping positions and lower-tipping casual restaurants, and second, even when they are fine dining servers and bartenders, customer bias results in workers of color earning less in tips. In other words, they earn far less money in tips and are therefore far less able to survive on the subminimum wage than their white counterparts.

The restaurant industry can be divided into three broad segments that vary markedly in terms of wages, working conditions, and workforce composition: fast-food or "quick-service"; casual full-service (including family-style and franchise); and fine dining (both casual fine dining and high-end "white tablecloth" establishments). Fast-food or quick-service restaurants provide limited table service and offer low-paying jobs to a workforce largely made up of workers of color, immigrants, and youth. Casual full-service, characterized by moderately priced meals and informal environments, includes both chain restaurants and franchises such as Olive Garden or Applebee's, and smaller, independently or family-owned establishments such as neighborhood restaurants. Fine dining is often defined by a price point per guest of $40 or more, including beverages, but excluding gratuity. A sizable percentage of the industry's growth can be attributed to casual fine dining, with an emphasis on high-quality food and service, and "white-tablecloth," which increasingly refers to upscale fine dining at a much higher price point. Fine dining establishments offer employment with the highest wages—especially via tips. Unsurprisingly, it is rare to find immigrants and people of color in these jobs. If they received One Fair Wage—a full minimum wage with tips on top—they could count on wage from their boss, rather than having their income wholly determined by the racial discrimination they face from both customers who tip them less and employers who keep them relegated to lesser-tipping industry segments and positions.

While a worker's ability to gain employment in a fine

dining establishment significantly increases her or his earnings potential, an equally important determinant is the type of position in the establishment itself. While many restaurants have their own internal structure of jobs and job titles, they typically range from managerial and supervisory positions, including general managers, assistant managers, wine directors/sommeliers, chefs, and sous-chefs; to front-of-the-house positions, which involve direct customer contact and include hosts, bussers, food runners, servers, captains, bartenders, and barbacks; and back-of-the-house positions, which involve no direct guest contact and include cleaners, dishwashers, prep cooks, line cooks, and chefs.

Most tipped workers work front of the house as servers, captains, and bartenders, and in fine dining restaurants they earn far more—sometimes two to five times more—than runners, bussers, and barbacks, which are the positions traditionally available to people of color. Khalid is a Moroccan immigrant who worked as a busser for many years before leaving the industry. He explains that the greater the pay and tips, the less likely people of immigrants and people of color are to hold those positions. "It's always like top management: white; serving management: 80 percent white. The busser, food runners, dishwashing people, the cook line, I can guarantee this is like 90 percent and above, is colored and immigrant people. As a person of color, you're not given the opportunity to advance. You have a low-level job, so that means by default you will get less tips, and it will affect your livelihood."

Restaurant workers experience poverty at twice the rate of workers overall, and as a result of the segregation Khalid describes, immigrants and other workers of color bear the brunt of this disparity—largely due to implicit bias by employers and customers.

As defined by the Kirwan Institute for the Study of Race and Ethnicity, implicit bias is the collection of "attitudes or stereotypes that affect our understanding, actions, and decisions in an unconscious manner. These biases are activated involuntarily and without an individual's awareness or intentional control." Though racial discrimination in hiring, retention, and promotion is common, it is rarely overtly expressed. Indeed, many restaurant owners are often unaware that common recruitment, hiring, and promotion practices are driving racial inequities and leading to employment barriers for immigrants and other workers of color. In order to test the effects of discrimination on employment, as co-director of the Restaurant Opportunities Centers United I led a matched pairs audit testing study; we sent more than four hundred pairs of evenly matched white people and people of color applicants into fine dining restaurants to see who would be hired for server positions. We found that white workers were more likely to be interviewed, and twice as likely to be hired, as equally or better-qualified workers of color.[4] When questioned, many employers attest that they are unable to find a sufficient number of quality applicants. Others defend the diversity of their workforce as a whole without taking into account the demographic differences by position and earning potential.[5]

In a series of focus groups, workers have observed that management already knows who it wants for a position, despite declaring that it is open for everyone. One worker noted, "The reality is, most of the time, it's not really open to everyone. They already know who they want. They just have to do it so they don't get in trouble." Orlando, a Black server with over a decade of experience, had been considered for a management role but was bypassed for a white coworker with less experience after a "drawn-out selection process." Another interviewee, a Latino male with fourteen years of experience as a server, was repeatedly asked to be a busser or expediter when he applied for server positions. "They would say, 'Would you rather be a busser or expediter? It might be easier for you?' I said, 'No, I'm here for the waiter position.' . . . The majority of servers at fine dining restaurants are men who are white or of European descent. Most of the Latinos will be hired only as busboys." Another male worker expressed his frustration: "There's not a position in the restaurant that I can't do, but . . . [hosts] or management always say, 'Oh, the kitchen is full right now.' . . . White people, even people of color, they always want to place me in the kitchen. . . . I am a waiter and I always have to explain what I'm looking for, and people always try to place me in the back, in the kitchen."

Immigrant women of color also have to contend with gendered expectations. Karina, who had ten years of experience as a runner, host, server, and cocktail waitress, said, "My first job was a serving job, and . . . I would apply for a server position, but then I would get put as a host. It wasn't because of a lack of experience. They would always put me as the host. . . . I had more experience running and bussing, and you can make more money doing that kind of stuff, but they just want the pretty girl hosting." Many workers shared a common experience of being required to train new, white workers for a higher-paid position but never being considered for that position themselves.

While qualified workers did object to being passed over for positions, many expressed a desire to avoid advancement opportunities in a form of "imposter syndrome," a common occurrence for immigrants, women, and people of color who do not fit the stereotypical image for certain positions. These workers said they did not want to pursue advancement out of concern they would be viewed as underqualified or "not the right fit" for the position, regardless of their actual skillset. Some workers who excluded themselves pointed to the discomfort of harmful racialized interactions with customers. Honor, a restaurant worker with four years' experience, explained why she did not want to work as a server: "I don't really like to interact with customers. . . . For example, I get questions like, 'Oh, you look so interesting. What are you?' Or 'What kind of accent is that? Where are you from?' All these questions that have nothing to do with what I'm doing."

Antonio, a server with four years' experience, has met many people unwilling to apply to fine dining positions. "'The standards are so high. I was intimidated to apply,' they say. . . . I'm blessed to be eloquent, but people are like, 'I [can't] last two minutes interviewing because I don't have a beautiful type of lingo. I can't talk . . . diplomatic.' They don't think they're up to par." Another worker noted, "I have a friend who is a busser, and I asked him if he wanted to be a server. It was his choice not to be a server. He thought his English was not good enough, but I never had a problem. . . . I just think that it's [workers of color] who want to stay where they are because they think that they're not good enough. I would say probably the number one barrier is racism, or because of communication issues. They don't fit the aesthetic of the restaurant. I've heard that before . . . speech and appearance."

Even those workers of color who did become servers felt the weight of guests' preferences for white staff. As one worker explained, "You could tell by the way they look at you as you're approaching the table. . . . After I greet them, and they hear how clear I speak, and how eloquent I am, I could see in their faces how mellowed out they get. I know that sometimes, when I'm in a [server] job, as a Black man

I have to comport myself in a way that puts white people largely at ease."[6] Customers were often condescending. As a worker said, "A lot of times I would come up to a table and feel like, because as a woman, and because I was brown, the assumption was that I didn't know my job. I got really sick of that after a while. Sick of people thinking I didn't know what I was talking about because I was a 'little brown girl.' . . . A really condescending kind of attitude and behavior because of my 'lack of knowledge.' They have no idea, if you're not one of them."

In July 2020, with the explosion of the Black Lives Matter movement, workers and employers began to push for serious change with regard to racial inequities in the restaurant industry. Industry stakeholders began to understand that anti-Black racism in the restaurant industry has affected all workers of color—including workers like Teto—and all workers and people—just as it has infected America more broadly. On August 20, Black Women's Equal Pay Day, One Fair Wage released a report showing that the national race and gender wage gap between tipped restaurant workers who are white men and Black women is $4.79 an hour. This gap was highest in New York and Massachusetts, which trailed only Alabama with the highest race and gender wage gaps in the nation, at $7.74 and $7.79 respectively. As self-proclaiming progressive leader states on race, Massachusetts and New York allow a race and gender wage gap in the restaurant industry that is 60 percent worse than the rest of the nation, largely due to the fact that these blue states persist with a subminimum wage for tipped workers. The report documented the fact that the race-gender wage gap can be entirely attributed to the fact that workers of color, and women of color in particular, are segregated into lower-tipping segments of the industry—casual rather than fine dining, confined to lower-tipping positions—and are bussers rather than servers and bartenders and tipped less even when they are working as servers and bartenders in fine dining restaurants. These already-existing disparities have been exacerbated by the COVID-19 pandemic, with all workers being asked to return to work for a subminimum wage and far less in tips.

In fact, the subminimum wage for tipped workers and this race and gender pay gap resulted in a horrific experience for tipped workers of color, and in particular Black tipped workers, during the pandemic. Combined survey data from our COVID-19 Service Workers' Emergency Relief Fund from multiple states indicated that while over 63 percent of all surveyed tipped workers from multiple states were either unable to obtain unemployment insurance benefits or uncertain if they qualified for unemployment insurance benefits, a much higher percentage—72 percent—of Black workers reported these same barriers to accessing unemployment insurance benefits. A staggering 95 percent of Black tipped service workers reported being unable or unsure whether they could afford their rent or mortgage, and 84 percent of Black tipped workers reported only being able to afford groceries for two weeks or less—all at much higher rates than their white counterparts. Upon returning to work, these workers faced both grave health risks and a subminimum wage for tipped workers when the majority of tipped workers surveyed from multiple states report that their tips are down at least 50 percent. This impact will be felt most by workers of color, who, because of customer bias, earn less in tips to begin with.

Fortunately, hundreds of independent restaurant owners observed these impacts and were moved by the murder of George Floyd and the ensuing demonstrations for racial justice to approach us about ending the subminimum wage for tipped workers. Responding to this desire for change during COVID-19, we worked with governors and mayors across the country to launch High Road Kitchens, which provided millions of dollars in cash grants to restaurant owners who committed to transitioning to One Fair Wage and undergoing our intensive Racial Equity Training Program. The popularity of the program and the number of restaurants voluntarily seeking to change their practices is a reflection of the new post-pandemic future that is possible for our industry—one that is racially equitable and sustainable for all stakeholders. Many of these employers have insisted that the industry simply cannot return to the inequitable systems that plagued it prior to the pandemic, but instead must reinvent itself. Clay Williams, co-founder of Black Food

Folks, an online service industry community, was quoted on December 31, 2020: "If a year from now the industry has gone back to business as usual and restaurant workers don't have livable wages, benefits, and protections, all of these 'Save Restaurants' campaigns will have been bullshit."

Around the time of Teto's departure from the Mexican restaurant, he began to realize how being undocumented also set him apart from some of his peers. "[I]t was my twenty-first birthday, and we were out at a club and we ended up in a scuffle. Well, I actually didn't throw any punches—I was breaking up the fight—and cops got called by the club. And we're being interviewed by cops, and I'm scared to death of getting arrested." He knew that while arrest could mean a night in jail for his friends, for Teto it might mean deportation and separation from his family. "I learned to think twice," he said. Everything he did had graver consequences than it did for his peers.

Nevertheless, Teto didn't let himself be daunted by his status. He was well-educated and he had years of experience working at restaurants; he was better equipped to find a better position in a restaurant—perhaps as a server, a bartender, or even a manager. At first, Teto was excited to find an opportunity to work as a bartender in an Italian restaurant in Tucson. Unfortunately, despite the new higher position, it did not take long for Teto to realize that something wasn't right. He was working five nights a week, but he wasn't being paid for five nights of work. "I saw my tips.

I was making over $200 a night. And I was only getting paid roughly $700 every two weeks, and supposedly my tips were already included in my paycheck." Teto asked his employer why he was seeing so little of the tips he was earning. "Well, I'm taxing you," came the reply. "You're taxing me how?" thought Teto. "And even then, if that's just my tips, then where's my hours?"

Teto started looking for another job. An opportunity arose at the Mexican restaurant company he had previously worked at, this time in a better position. The company had a new restaurant location with a different manager. After having worked as a bartender in the other restaurant, he was able to come back to the company as a bartender, earning between $800 and $1,000 a week in tips. Initially, Teto thought it was one of the best jobs he'd ever had. The restaurant, now into its second year, was doing very well. "I had a sense of security while working with them," he said.

After several months, something horrible happened—he was accused of stealing. "There was a manager code for voids, for checking the tips, for checking sales and stuff like that, which I had. The owner knew that I had it. He and his wife would go in, they would eat, they would drink, then at the end instead of paying their tab, they would tell me, 'Just delete and void our tab.' So I would do it."

This arrangement ended up getting Teto into trouble. Later, when he and a manager had a disagreement over the number of hours Teto had worked, the voids Teto had inputted for the owner and his wife resurfaced. "The manager said I was 'basically pocketing cash.' They said that I did it, that I would delete or void the tabs and keep the cash."

He left that job. "After that happened, I went through a rough patch. All of 2017 was a really, really rough year for me," he recalled. "I went from making $800 to $1,000 a week working there to my lowest point getting paid $8 an hour, working twenty hours a week." Teto feels that his immigration status had everything to do with the way he was treated. "They see this twenty-two-year-old kid who is an immigrant that doesn't have legal status. How is he going to sue me?" Teto was at rock bottom. "Financially, I struggled a lot. Emotionally, because I was struggling financially. I had never felt so undocumented until 2017. That's when my reality hit me. I'm not here legally. I can't leave a workplace like a citizen can or a resident can and go find another job as easily. Here, I'm going to struggle three or four times more."

Teto ended up moving from low-wage job to low-wage job. "It's easier as an illegal immigrant to find a job in a restaurant, in the hospitality industry, whether it be cleaning theaters at night or working as housekeeping in a hotel or cleaning houses or working back of house in a restaurant or working as a server. Those are the easiest jobs to find."

He worked at an IHOP, which he didn't like, then at a hotel. "I worked there for about a week and it just wasn't for me. It was too far." Again his undocumented status was a factor in where he worked: "I felt like I was also exposing myself to too much. In Tucson, if you are within city limits, and you are dealing with the police departments, you're fine, but once you deal with sheriffs, you start to go into a tricky area. I typically don't like working in areas where I have to drive and go through sheriff territory."

Teto finally landed a catering job with a responsible employer. "She honestly paid me what she could. She was not at all taking advantage of my situation. She was only paying me $8 an hour and giving me about twenty hours a week. She really helped me out." Unexpectedly, he experienced something that he had not experienced during all those years working as a busser or any of the other jobs he had worked at. "I started to feel valued again. She saw who I was. She would tell me, 'Hey, this is for only a little while. You know, if you find something better, I understand, I want you to do better.' I was making about $200 a week, and it was as if I were making $1,000. She was a very good boss." He knew that she couldn't pay him more. "It was a brand new business. She didn't have much clientele, but she needed somebody to help her out because she was a mother with kids who had opened a business and she needed somebody to help her. I didn't mind helping her out; she helped me out." And she helped him to feel valued in other ways: "She gave me Christmas presents. I would eat for free there. Sometimes, if she made food at her house, she would bring me food. It was the little details."

She looked out for him. "Even on the days that I didn't work, she would call me, 'Hey, I have a catering event, come on, put your clothes on, work it with me, I'll pay you a little bit more, you'll make tips.' And she had a couple of friends that own bars, and they had a couple of events and I bartended them. I saw her willingness to help me, and she restored my faith that there are good people out there. Maybe they can't pay you a million bucks, but with the little bit that they can give you, you're earning it in an honest and ethical way. It's not about the money. It's about being valued, being respected, and feeling appreciated."

Teto feels that much of the lack of respect he has encountered at so many different places of work is a common experience among immigrant restaurant workers in Tucson. "We're definitely a demographic that is taken advantage of. There are some places where you only get your tips. You don't get paid hourly, or they pay you less than hourly. Or here's a hundred dollars a week type deal. Sometimes tips really depend on sales."

Whenever he applies for a new job, Teto wonders how his immigration status will be used against him. "If anything happens, am I going to be the first one to go?" It's especially precarious because, when he isn't being paid in cash, he has to use another person's social security number to work in certain places. He recalled one particular job: "I was using somebody else's social security number, a friend of mine's, and he was still fighting his immigration case.

He was working construction, getting paid cash. He told me, 'Hey, I know you're struggling, you can use mine,' as a friend helping me out." Teto didn't feel comfortable using the social security number for long and so he resigned. "It was a really well-paying job, a manager position, [but I left] because I didn't know what was going to happen with him."

For another job, he used his uncle's social security number. "Me and him look a lot alike, so there weren't really questions asked. They know that they're hiring people like you. It's basically a don't ask, don't tell situation."

At one of the restaurants Teto was working at, he was treated well, but again he ran into the same issues over his status. The person whose identity he was using called him to tell him that he had been ordered to leave the country in a month: "Hey, I have to leave by January, by December 31, sorry. I need you to put your two weeks in at work." Teto went to the manager to tell him that he had to resign. "Can I know why?" asked the manager. "It's not because I'm not happy here," Teto told him. "It's not because I don't want to work here. I'm very thankful. I'm making really good money." But he had to tell him that he had lied on his application. "I'm not this person. I'm somebody else, I am still the same employee, but I don't have the status." The manager told him to "take the time that you need to work here. If you have more time, let me know." On his final day, the owner approached him and said, "When you fix your status, come and the manager position is waiting for you."

For the first time in a long while he has hope that despite the uncertainties of an immigrant without permission to work, he can get by on his skills. "I'm someone that once I start working somewhere, I move up really fast. They see my work ethic, they see how strong of a server I am. They see how well my customer service is." But he is still dependent on the kindness of his employers. "I've been very lucky and very blessed in some way with the people I have come across that do know my status, that are people that are willing to help me out. My current bosses know my situation, but they still decided to give me a job. I'm super thankful for them, for the first time in a long time, I feel like regardless of my status, as long as I am the employee that I know that I am, I will have my job."

Moreover, the original Mexican restaurant that kept him as a busser for eight years and then later accused him of theft has finally recognized his value and invited him to come back as a server. Teto remains eternally positive. "It doesn't matter how low you are. There's always a light at the end of the tunnel. Always. Always. If you are somebody who is hard-working and you don't give up, you will come out on top again."

4

Dia and Adrinne

Parking and Airport Attendants for a Living Wage

"A lot of people think our job is easy"

Dia King was born at Providence Hospital in northeast Washington, DC. His mother was an African American woman who grew up in New York; her family had migrated to New York from Arkansas. Dia's mother had left New York in the 1960s to escape her father and experience the burgeoning Black power movement in Washington, DC; she came at the age of eighteen to go to Howard University.

Dia's father, for his part, was a tailor from Barbados. "He was an immigrant who wanted to make it big in America." Dia's father ran with people in high places—when he needed a green card, DC mayor Marion Barry was the one to sign the paperwork. "So I partly have to thank Marion Barry for my life," says Dia. "Without him, my father wouldn't have been able to stay in the country, and my parents would have never met."

Shortly after Dia's parents got together, Dia's mother gave

birth to Dia and his twin brother in 1972. But they didn't stay together long. "By the time we were two or three years old they broke up, and we were on public assistance. My mom started working at the post office to get off public assistance." Dia, his twin brother, and his mother went to live with a friend that Dia's mother met at the post office.

With a new steady job, Dia's mother was finally able to get an apartment for their family in southeast Washington, DC, and then not long after that, she was able to move the family to a townhouse in Landover, and then finally a house in Andrews Village near Andrews Air Force base. His mother then got interested in accounting and went to school to be an accountant. After several tries and lots of encouragement from her sons, she finally got her license to be a certified public accountant and started working for a nonprofit broadcasting organization. She ended up buying several homes for the family, until she got caught up in the subpar mortgage crisis that hit African Americans the worst. Still, she had gotten work, gone to school, become a CPA and a property owner—all as a single mother raising two young sons.

"My mom raised us great. We were working class, but we never went without anything to eat. The electricity got turned off just once. We always had great Christmases, and we never felt like we didn't have enough because Mom never let us feel that way." Still, Dia would notice little things from time to time that gave him an inkling of how she struggled to maintain the family. "I noticed she put the phone bill in our name. She hid a lot of stuff from us—she didn't want the kids to see that she didn't have enough money. On those Christmases she wouldn't pay a bill in order to get us Christmas gifts. So her credit was bad. I learned that most single moms don't have great credit because they're always hustling."

Meanwhile, Dia's mother struggled to give her boys the best education she could. "We were in and out of so many different schools because my mom wanted to give us the best education, but she couldn't afford it. We were in and out of private and public schools, maybe ten to fifteen schools, some very influential. We went to Sidwell Friends, School Without Walls, and St. Andrews in Bethesda, where Donald Trump's son is going to now. . . . We had to get up three to four hours before our friends to take the bus to Potomac

Avenue, the Metro to Bethesda, and then the bus to a school where they treated us like garbage. She thought she was doing the best she could." Eventually, Dia and his brother came back to the local public schools.

Dia started working right after high school as an AT&T relay operator for deaf people. "I was the go between—this was before technology. They'd call me on a text telephone. I would say what they typed to the person they were calling, then I would type the response back to them." Dia had been with AT&T for twelve years when technology shook up the business and he was laid off for a year.

Following his layoff, Dia worked in a variety of odd jobs for several years. In 2011 he met union organizers outside a grocery store who were organizing around good jobs in DC. Dia signed up to volunteer. "They took me to my first action on Verizon, which wasn't paying its fair share of taxes. They trained me to canvass for Obama." After volunteering for a while, an SEIU (Service Employees International Union) organizer heard that Dia needed a job and hired him. "I was the roadie—during actions, I'd rent a van, go get the supplies, pick people up and bring them to actions."

In 2014, Dia went to see a DC job counselor, who presented him with the possibility of being a parking valet. Dia attended a hiring event at a hotel and was hired on the spot after a drug test. "I was hired by a parking company—a valet company for a lot of hotels in the area. It does the parking for hotel chains in downtown DC. The hotels usually have their own garage, but sometimes another company owns the garage. There are places where the garage is under the building, other places where the parking lot is a few blocks down the street."

As he started working as a parking valet at various hotels, he began to understand that many hotels wanted the parking valets to look as though they were employees of the hotel, but did not want to hire the valets directly, preferring to subcontract to the parking company. "The hotels don't want the responsibility [of hiring you]. But they want all of the valets to look like their own employees. They want you to look like you work for the hotel."

Dia believes this deception is unfortunate because "working for [the parking company] is different than working for the hotel. The [hotel] treats its employees very well. I go to the cafeteria, and there are signs that say, 'We love our employees.' I've never felt that way about my company. The reason I keep doing it is that I like the hotel I'm working in."

Parking valets like Dia earn the subminimum wage for tipped workers in over forty states and Washington, DC. "When I first got this kind of job, I thought, because it was mostly tips, it would be more lucrative. When you get tips people automatically think you'll make a killing. But in reality . . . my checks kind of suck."

As with other workers earning the subminimum wage for tipped workers, Dia is supposed to earn enough tips to make up the difference between the subminimum wage and the regular minimum wage, or the company is supposed to make up the difference. "I started at $7 an hour. In order to earn the minimum wage of $12, I had to make $5 in tips every hour extra to get it up to minimum wage. There were days when I made more than that . . . and days when I made less. The paycheck was extra. I used tips to pay most of the bills."

Unfortunately, the tips fluctuated wildly. "The tips went up and down—depending on holidays, tips would go down. Depending on the weather, tips would go down. In DC, a lot of the economy depends on Congress being in office. When congressmembers are not around, our tips go down. None of the congressmembers are around over the summer."

The weather also made it difficult to stay outside, waiting to park people's cars. "We'd be working out in the element. Once I was at a hotel at 13th Street. It was thunder-storming and raining, but they want you to stand and look a certain way. We were huddled by heaters. The hotel lobby manager came out and yelled at us, made us stand up in the rain 'posted up,' arms folded, waiting for cars to come in. It was raining like crazy—but we had to go post up, go stand up. It was humiliating."

In 2018, after four years of work as a parking valet, Dia was volunteering at a local organization called One DC when an organizer from the Restaurant Opportunities Center (ROC) came to explain Initiative 77. Initiative 77 was a recently passed ballot measure in Washington, DC, to raise the minimum wage for tipped workers to the full minimum wage of $15 an hour, with tips on top. Initiative 77 had passed overwhelmingly; nevertheless, the Washington, DC, City Council was threatening to overturn the measure with a massive lobbying and disinformation campaign funded by the National Restaurant Association. To explain their reasoning in overturning such a popular ballot measure, Council leadership used the offensive and patronizing argument that the people of DC did not understand what they were voting for.

The ROC organizer asked Dia if he would come testify at the City Council hearing where members were considering overturning Initiative 77, and Dia agreed.

Following his testimony, Dia was featured multiple times on the local news. "I was on TV again that night, and the next Wednesday after that, my boss pulled me into the office and told me they were giving me a raise. It was my first raise in four years of work. I asked her, 'Is it because I was on TV?' She said no, but it was clear that someone higher up had called her."

"It shows that organizing does work," Dia said. "It took me being on TV to get a raise after four years!"

Dia continues to fight for One Fair Wage in Washington, DC, but has also become a national leader among tipped workers. He has attended national convenings, meeting tipped workers from other states. "I met another worker from New York who has a family and had to take time off from work to come to the conference."

From those experiences, Dia has developed the belief that he has a responsibility to continue to organize. "I'm able to do this. I'm in a unique position. I know that the world needs to be better, and I'm in a unique position to fight. I know there aren't that many forty-seven-year-olds that are single and don't have a mortgage. I could show up almost anywhere with a week's notice. The average person working these jobs can't just take a break."

Dia feels there is so much to fight for. "We're not recognizing our full potential because we're not united. We need to be more united. "It's Bizzaro World—it's backward, our world is backward. How is it that the 1 percent are able to control the 99 percent—it's against physics! It works because they keep us divided. Once we unite the 99 percent, we can absorb the 1 percent and make it the full world it's supposed to be."

Adrinne Hicks is an airport valet at the Houston Airport who was born and raised in Houston, Texas. She was raised by her single grandmother, a strong woman who served as a role model for Adrinne for the rest of her life. "My grandma was strong-willed and determined. My grandma is the first thing of God. She taught me that anything you stand for, you fight for. She would tell me, 'If you feel like someone is doing you wrong, you need to stand up, not just for yourself, but for others. What you can handle, others can't handle, they will break.'" This strength rubbed off on Adrinne early on. "I was like a little boy growing up—I would fight quick. Later I learned to turn that energy toward helping others."

Adrinne watched her grandmother become a self-made entrepreneur and a leader in the Black community. "My grandma was clear. She divorced my grandpa, and as she always was a hard worker, she worked and saved, and eventually bought her own eighteen-wheeler [truck], and hired someone to work it. She had her head on." Adrinne's grandmother was able to earn enough income through her trucking business to support the family, something that Adrinne struggles to do in her airport valet position today.

Adrinne faced challenges growing up. She became a single mother with her first daughter as a teenager, and her second at twenty years old. "I didn't have my parents and didn't have a father. I learned not to need anything from a man. . . . I faced ups and downs, highs and lows. I just need to keep pressing. Through various trials and tribulations, I get strength through the storm. It feels like a torment when going through it, but I always ask what did I need to learn from that situation." Adrinne's strength and her grandmother's example allowed her to make it through school even with her daughter. "I graduated from high school and went to community college for medical billing and coding, but I didn't want to do that work."

Over several decades, Adrinne worked several different

jobs. In 2019, she was hired by a company called ABM as a skycap, taking luggage from passengers curbside and pushing passengers in wheelchairs at the Houston Airport, earning $2.13 an hour plus tips. Now older, with three grown children, Adrinne found it to be challenging work for very little pay. "It's lots of wear and tear on your body. Luggage is up to seventy to eighty pounds. You use your feet, legs, and arms; it's very physical work. But nothing else was calling. I'm a single mother of three, and I had to take what was there at the time to provide for my babies." As Adrinne got to meet her peers in the new job, she was shocked at the pay and working conditions. "I've seen a lot, how long the people have been working there. Wow, you can stay at a job thirty years making $2.13. Some people they get stuck."

"Skycaps are hard workers. We wheelchair people, coming from the gate, all the way down. It's a long walk. We could be pushing people who are overweight. It's also hard mental work. People come up and ask tons of questions. I had to learn quick about the whole airport, International to Domestic. People [might be] running late and need help with all their luggage. I need to get them there. Many people are coming from around the world and don't speak English. I problem solve with them. I have them write it down, [and then I have to] find other people on staff to translate this and that. A lot of people think our job is easy, but you need to have an open mind there."

Recently, Adrinne noticed that skycaps have an additional

immense burden that they are not trained or supported to deal with. "We need to pay attention to human trafficking. Recently, [I saw] this girl looking like she is uncomfortable, she won't talk to me, she is looking down. I had to tell the police. I found out that she is being trafficked. You always have to be aware and alert there. There is a lot of movement [of people], twenty-four hours a day."

Adrinne's coworkers at the airport are diverse in every sense of the word. "It is really mixed in terms of who works [as a] skycap. There are lots of Asians, Nigerians, African Americans, whites. That's what I like about ABM, they will give anyone an opportunity to work." Nevertheless, it is hard to build community given the high rates of worker turnover. "The turnover rate is heavy, 'cause it's too much work for not getting paid. The airport is open twenty-four hours a day, seven days a week—they need workers all the time. They are constantly hiring."

Adrinne points primarily to the wage of $2.13 an hour as the source of the high turnover. "Of course we should get paid $12 an hour when they make billions. People can't afford a car, they take the bus, or have a car but can't afford the gas. I have to drive thirty-five minutes every day—that's a lot of mileage and gas that's needed, and then I have to pay to park. I can't afford healthcare coverage, and then I get penalized at the end of the year. Everyone is not lazy and staying at home. We get up every day. We work Christmas and Thanksgiving, and don't get any time and a half. But the people who own the airport are at home with their families on Christmas while we are working for $2.13 an hour to make the airport run." In Adrinne's case, she wasn't able to celebrate Christmas because she didn't have the money.

Living off the variability and instability of tips is challenging for Adrinne. She almost got evicted but was able to get an extension. "Mentally it's draining. You try not to worry about what is going to happen and keep the faith. But what if I can't make it? The holidays are over, I only made $30 yesterday in tips. My light bill is $200. No healthcare. I have necessities. My baby has an afterschool program I need to pay for. My older boy is a senior [in high school], he has prom, senior trip. Their fathers aren't in their lives. . . . He isn't helping, I got to let that go and keep moving."

Earning $2.13 an hour was a shock to Adrinne, compared to her previous jobs. "I don't know how people can live on $2.13 all their life. I was getting paid $13 at my last job. Before that I was working for myself selling an inspirational clothing line. In terms of customers, you have people who have a heart, who fly all the time, who know how little we get paid, who will give you a $25 tip, but that is one in a hundred people. Some people ask if they can tip you, and I let them know yes, we work off of tips. I try to educate them. But most people just give you $2 or $3, some don't give anything. They just don't know. One customer did not believe that we were paid $2.13. They said that must be untrue, that would be abusing the law, there is no way."

Since they are all so dependent on tips to earn the minimum wage to feed their families, Adrinne's peers all have different views about customer service and whether they should push for tips, and vary their service based on the tips. "Me, I love helping people. If I see a single mother with three or four bags, I'll help you, you don't have to give me anything. At the end of the day, God sees your heart and He will reward you later. You never know who you['re] helping and why you['re] helping. I may see someone disabled, and I would want someone to help my grandma, [to say] 'Let me help you to the car,' with their cane and wheelchair. [But] different people have different perspectives, [some] won't do anything if they are not getting paid [from tips]. But I don't work like that." Some of Adrinne's coworkers indicate that because they're not actually getting a wage other than tips, they do not feel obligated to serve if they are not tipped. These differing views seemingly contradict the National Restaurant Association's argument that paying tipped workers a full minimum wage, rather than having a subminimum wage and forcing these workers to rely on tips, would reduce the quality of customer service.

Adrinne notes that there is also a hierarchy between the airport and airline workers, who earn salaries and benefits, and the subcontracted skycap workers who work for $2.13 an hour—even though the skycap workers ultimately serve the airport and airline passengers. "Well, I'm a newbie there. It was hard to get hired on with United [Airlines]. They don't really hire like that—they open up hiring every ten years. I would love to work for the actual airport to get the benefits, healthcare, 401k. Since we contract with ABM, we work hard for United. But we don't get any of those benefits."

Quite often the $2.13 wage does not even cover the cost for Adrinne to get to work. "One thing that really gets me is that we have to pay to park. We're paying $25 a week to park, $50 out of my check. We should park for free. Why should we have to pay to park? It's a no-win situation. We bring in so much money and then they are taking money out of our check just to work for them. The politicians need to do something about this."

In fact, Adrinne has been organizing with SEIU, the Service Employees International Union, to raise the minimum wage for tipped skycap workers. "We protest in front of the airport. There have been protests all over the country, and those people are getting $10 plus tips. Why are we still stuck at $2.13? Why is the mayor not putting pressure on to make the airport actually pay us?" Adrinne feels the lack of action on the part of elected officials on the issue of the subminimum wage discourages young people from voting again. "Minorities and younger people came out and voted [for the mayor], so you need to do something about it. People complain about young people not coming out to vote. Our older generation didn't have any choice about it. You know if you are a minority, when we come out to vote we want action, we need action. Older generations fought for rights, but then nothing happened, so it's no wonder that the younger generations don't think anything will happen." In her case, Adrinne and her fellow skycaps worked with the union to mobilize each other to vote as a way to send elected officials a message. "You know we went out to vote. At least sixty people at the airport we all went together."

The fight is personal to Adrinne—she knows her employer is profiting off her hard work and low wages, and that the ridiculously low wages have meant that wages for working people—including in her own family—have eroded over time. "ABM has a contract because the workers bring their skills and hard work. We make the money for the airport. Back then they were making more than we are making now. My grandma's generation were making more than we make on $2.13. If that's not slavery, I don't know what is. That's slavery, period. Your life is in someone else's hands." With her grandmother's spirit, Adrinne is committed to keep fighting for One Fair Wage with her fellow workers. "We are strong. Together we are stronger. Everyone must do their part. . . . I never want to settle in life."

5

Yenelia

Nail Salon Technicians Struggling to Get By

"The customers don't say thank you, but they want perfection"

Yenelia, a nail salon worker, is a member of Workers United, one of several nail salon workers' rights organizations that form the Nail Salon Workers' Coalition of New York. Yenelia is from a small town by the sea in Honduras. She grew up as one of five children; her father, a fisherman, supported all of the family and the kids' education from income from fishing. "Thanks to him, I got an education. I got a degree in business. But I was never able to get a job—my mother and father supported me the whole time I was there, because there were no jobs in Honduras."

After getting her education, Yenelia got pregnant with her first child, a boy. But when her son turned two, her father came to the family with an opportunity: he could support Yenelia or one of her siblings to go to the United States, to be able to work and send money home to the family. A great discussion erupted over who would be the person to go. "This responsibility fell to me because, according to my parents, it was me who was going to be able to support them," Yenelia said. "I had to leave behind my son, who was two years old. When I crossed the border, I had a surprise. I was pregnant again. It was very difficult—I didn't know the language or the system. But I moved forward. I started working in a nail salon. I gave birth to my son and decided to send him home to Honduras after eight months. I couldn't pay for babysitting and also send home money for my other baby."

After some time in the United States, Yenelia met someone and had three more children—now she had a total of four children in the United States and one back home in Honduras. "When I first came I thought it was good; at least I had a job I couldn't get back home. But there also was never enough money. When I first arrived and changed the currency to send home, it seemed like a lot. But then when I started actually living here, I realized you can't pay the rent, you can't spend time with your kids. You work when you're sick, but no matter what you do the money doesn't stretch to pay the bills. You don't have a life—you're always running."

When Yenelia first arrived, she thought she'd be cleaning houses. "My aunt, who lives in New York, said 'Everyone is working in nail salons. Just go to our friends' house—they'll teach you.' So I went, and I learned. The thing is that it was something I never liked to get done for myself—my nails. But necessity obligates you. I learned on the job in two months. When I had a baby the owner fired me, so I got another nail salon job."

*   *   *

In her first nail salon job, Yenelia did not really know what she was doing, but desperately needed to work. "The boss said she wanted a nail technician, so I lied. I said yes, I know how to do nails. I think I had gotten my nails done twice in my life. On my first day, when I started working, she was behind me, and I was trembling. But I kept working. Fear and necessity make you do things you never think you're going to do. And when I got my first paycheck there, and it was $450 per week, it was glorious. I thought, 'I'm going to keep this job.'"

With a steady job with long hours, Yenelia had to make the painful decision to send each of her children back to Honduras when they were a few months old, and then bring them back to the United States when they were a little older. "I didn't have enough money to pay the rent, let alone to pay babysitters. Even when I tried to pay it was painful—the babies learn to love the babysitters more than you, because you drop them off really early, and you come to get them 10 or 11 p.m. at night. They weren't growing up with me. Then there's the babysitters—they don't watch them well. So I made the decision to send them back home. After they turned five years old I brought them back to the United States—then I thought I could take care of them. They could go to school in the United States. I wanted them to learn English."

Almost all of the women we met with Yenelia were mothers who had left children behind in their home country, like her. "It was really hard to leave them," one told us, "because as a mother, you want to protect them. But I had to leave them alone. They were with my sisters, but they had their own kids to worry about." Like Yenelia, they all also missed their parents and family. Another nail salon worker, Araceli, told us, "It's very hard to be very far from family. Things mark you. It's the worst."

Yenelia works on commission, taking "tickets" from her employer to work on clients' nails. Her employer makes money off of every client interaction. Yenelia's meager commission is supplemented by meager tips. "Sometimes I worked full days, and I get like $2 or $5 in tips. Sometimes you have lots of clients, like on a Friday, you'll work a lot. Other days it's just $5 in tips, or nothing. There's no good reason for your wage to depend on tips. It's not the obligation of the clients to pay you—it's the obligation of the employer. People who come to get their nails done bring the exact amount needed to get their nails done—they don't bring extra for tips."

Nail salon workers can be paid the subminimum wage for tipped workers in forty-three states. Several of Yenelia's fellow nail salon workers expressed frustration at the fact that the subminimum wage and meager tips do not add up. "I love my work. Not because of the money—I studied to be a cosmetologist. But it's unjust—you kill yourself working.

The customers don't say thank you, but they want perfection. They don't even give $5 for perfection."

"The employer pays $11 [per hour] including tips. They make us sign what hour we came, what hour we left. And they calculate that based on when you sit down with your first client, and when you get up from the last client. But I still have to clean up. And then they ask you to put down what you earned in tips. I don't do that. You rely on the tips, but the tips aren't guaranteed."

Like restaurant and other tipped subminimum wage workers, nail salon workers receive a subminimum wage in most states that have a subminimum wage for tipped workers. This means that the employer may legally pay the subminimum wage—still $2.13 at the federal level—and tips left by customers are meant to bring the worker to the full minimum wage. The employer is supposed to ensure that tips make up the difference between the subminimum wage and the regular minimum wage or pay the worker the difference if they do not, but as in the restaurant industry, employers actually complying with this rule in nail salons are nearly nonexistent. Regardless of whether they do or not, because of the subminimum wage for tipped workers, as in restaurants, tips left by nail salon customers do not add to the wage—they replace it.

The tips are also seasonal. Yenelia explains, "For women who do manicures and pedicures, they're busy in the summertime. For people who do regular nails, they're busy at other times." But all the women agree that January and February are the worst months. One of the women calls those months "fatal."

Most pay and tips are given to Yenelia and her coworkers in cash. When tips are processed on a credit card, just like in the restaurant industry, the employer will take a cut of the workers' tips for credit card processing fees. So Yenelia and all her fellow workers prefer cash.

Of course, all of the women know their rights are being violated. One recounted being in her nail salon when the Department of Labor came in to investigate. "The boss wrote down that they were paying us more, but it was a lie. Really they were paying us $55 in cash per day. There might be tips, but the salary never went up above $55 per day. So they made us lie to the Department of Labor. When the investigators asked, we said, 'Yes they give us the uniform for free,' but in fact they charge us. We said we work six days a week. But in truth they didn't want to give us a day off. There were some things that I tried to tell the truth about, even though they had told us to lie. I told them that after six days they still pay us the same, no overtime." This nail salon closed soon after the investigation.

In one week in early May 2015, a series of *New York Times* articles exposed the ugly underside of the booming nail salon industry. Getting one's "nails done" had become routine among an increasing number of people across economic and demographic spectrums, making nail care the fastest-growing sector in the beauty industry.[1] The U.S. nail salon industry is a burgeoning sector with over $8.5 billion in revenue in 2017.[2] In the last eight years, the industry has experienced a 33 percent increase in revenue and in the last twenty-five years has seen the number of salons more than triple.[3] Currently, there are an estimated 5,569 nail salons in New York, 2,000 of which are in New York City.[4]

The sector's growth is also reflected in the ballooning workforce. The number of manicurists and pedicurists in New York grew to 18,370 workers in 2017, a 17 percent increase over the previous four years.[5] Since 2011, the number of workers in dedicated nail salons has grown by 92 percent. Increased consumer demand for nail services means the sector is expected to continue to grow.[6] There are currently 30,538 active nail specialty licenses in New York, and by 2024, the nail salon workforce in New York is expected to expand an additional 22.4 percent.[7]

The *New York Times* series also uncovered a longstanding truth about this luxury sector: in major metropolitan areas it is almost entirely staffed by undocumented immigrant women with little or no rights and who are routinely exploited by their employers—and by customers who demand perfection and leave little in tips. Despite being the single largest population of licensed professionals in the United States, nail salon technicians often work long hours in hazardous conditions and are paid a subminimum wage that leaves them dependent on tips to make ends meet.[8] This combination, compounded with the seasonal nature of the work in New York, routinely leaves nail salon workers earning below the state minimum wage.

Though the median wage for nail salon workers in New York is $9.94, New York City nail salon workers are routinely paid a day rate ranging from $35 to $80, and in some extreme cases as low as $30, before tips for workdays often exceeding ten hours.[9] Interviews conducted by the *New York Times* with over one hundred nail salon workers uncovered "rates of pay so low that the so-called tip calculation is virtually meaningless."[10] Overtime pay is also virtually nonexistent for workers, even though the average nail salon worker in New York City works forty-five hours a week and, in some cases, up to eighty-four hours a week.[11] Furthermore, since nail salon work is seasonal in New York, workers are left at the mercy of massive fluctuations in income. Still, even during the slow winter months, workers are expected to be at the salon for over forty hours a week and are usually not compensated by owners, as required by law, when their earnings including tips fall short of the full minimum wage.

The abysmal working conditions and subminimum wages in the nail salon industry perpetuate economic insecurity among its workforce. Nail salon workers in New York live in poverty at 2.5 times the rate of New York's overall workforce.[12] Additionally, the typical setup in nail salons exposes workers to a harmful environment, where breaks and proper protective and ergonomic equipment are not provided. This creates an additional financial burden on workers, as their fluctuating income often puts them in the position of having to choose between addressing health issues that arise from their working conditions and paying their bills.

The subminimum wage has helped institutionalize wage theft as a nail salon industry norm. In 2015 the New York State Department of Labor conducted compliance sweeps in nail salons, finding rampant labor abuses, including pervasive wage and hour violations.[13] As of late 2015, all but 12 of the 230 salons investigated were cited for violating at least one labor law.[14] The sweep also found that 85 percent of nail salons failed to maintain adequate payroll records, making it the most common citation.[15] In some of the more egregious instances, nail technicians were forced to work for no pay or had to pay salon owners a fee; several owners admitted to presenting fake payroll records to deceive labor investigators.[16] Lack of recordkeeping in many instances also meant that workers were left with the burden of calculating their employer's compliance with the tip penalty regulations. By the end of the investigation, more than 40 percent of the salons had been cited for underpaying employees, and the New York State Department of Labor ordered them to pay $1.1 million in back wages and several hundred thousand dollars in damages.[17]

As with the restaurant industry, the negative impacts of the subminimum wage system in the nail salon industry disproportionately impact women. In New York, 87 percent of nail salon workers are women and 72 percent are foreign-born.[18] Most nail salon workers are also mothers—over half are mothers and 37 percent of them are single moms.[19] The tip penalty—tips cutting against workers' wages—also institutionalized a gender pay gap, as women in nail salons earn 25 percent less than men, resulting in a $200,000 lifetime gender tax.[20] Women in nail salons are dependent on tips for a bigger portion of their income than men are, and, as a result, are more vulnerable to poverty and economic insecurity.

The *New York Times* series exposed all of these injustices—the daily trafficking of immigrant women to work ten- and twelve-hour days in nail salons across major metropolitan areas; not being paid the minimum wage or having tips stolen; being verbally and physically abused; and struggling with childcare working long hours. Nail salon workers can be paid the subminimum wage for tipped workers in forty-three states, and most workers reported to the *Times* that no employer ever paid them the full minimum wage when tips did not materialize to bring them the full minimum wage.

The *New York Times* series launched a massive outcry and policy response. As mentioned above, the New York State Department of Labor had initiated an investigation into nail salons; the New York City Office of Labor Policy and Standards conducted "sweeps" of nail salons, informing workers of their rights and employers of the law. New York State promised partnership with immigrant workers' organizations focused on nail salon workers. "Healthy" nail salons were uplifted and recognized for using green chemicals. Many workers' stories were told, some nail salons were shut down, and many, many workers learned their rights.

But one thing remains the same: nail salon workers still receive the subminimum wage for tipped workers. As immigrants, they continue to feel disempowered to fight against abuse of the two-tiered wage system; many employers continue to dock workers' tips and almost none ensure that tips bring workers to the full minimum wage. As a result, nail salon worker organizations like Workers United in Queens have joined forces with other sectors of subminimum wage workers to fight for One Fair Wage. These workers and their representatives realize that, rather than simply increasing enforcement of their rights to ensure that their tips bring them to the full minimum wage, it will be more effective to require that their employers pay them a full minimum wage, like most other workers, with tips on top.

And then there are the chemicals. Yenelia feels guilty that she worked with the chemicals during her pregnancy. "I think it affected my children. My children were born with bronchitis. I think it was the chemicals where I work—I worked the whole nine months and when I was in labor. And now I have developed allergies to the chemicals. I only learned to take care of myself through the organization."

Yenelia's fellow workers agreed that their children were affected by nail salon chemicals while in the womb. "I worked while I was pregnant," one of them added, "and my child had problems in school; he was different. He was diagnosed with ADHD. No doctor said this, but I think it was because of the chemicals I worked with while I was pregnant. I know a lot of my coworkers' kids have asthma and learning problems. I have a lot of guilt for exposing my children to those chemicals."

Yenelia and her fellow workers note that the exposure to chemicals is exacerbated by the long hours, lack of breaks, and lack of protective equipment. "It's affected me—the long hours, not enough time to go to the bathroom or eat. We have to eat our food quickly and keep working. You spend six days working, and there's not enough time to eat. They get annoyed if we sit to eat—we have to go back to work. It's also affected my vision—the lights of the machines—I don't have glasses or anything. No protective equipment. When I'm putting gel on people's nails, I do six people in a row and I get tears in my eyes. There's dust in the salon and I can't breathe the same. It has affected me, because we don't have protective equipment."

Yenelia's experiences of chemical exposure and its impacts unfortunately are not unique; the impacts of these still-unregulated chemicals are beginning to get documented. In 2014, *Scientific American* featured a piece detailing four key unregulated chemicals that pose serious danger to workers, including respiratory problems and birth defects. In 2019, an NIH-funded study of Temple University academics examined over one hundred nail salon workers' exposure to three toxic chemicals and found that workers reported several health problems that were created or exacerbated by working in the nail salon industry, including headaches (8 percent); lightheadedness (9.8 percent); and irritation to the nose, eyes, throat, and skin (21.2 percent). The study noted that "approximately 70 percent of participants reported that they had been pregnant, 11.7 percent of whom had at least one miscarriage." This data shows that government regulation is needed to ensure the safety of both workers and customers.

Those nail salon workers who work on commission like Yenelia have to be willing to work in all kinds of different places with inadequate facilities, leading to any number of physical complications. "You get back pain because there are no chairs, you're sitting on the floor and there's not enough light. You develop allergies and gastritis from the products. There's no time to get water, no time to go to the bathroom. Sometimes you don't want to drink water so that you don't have to go to the bathroom later."

One of Yenelia's fellow workers told a story of a coworker who became very ill working in the nail salon. "Back in January, my friend fell sick. She went to hospital, and they told her her lung had collapsed. She spent two or three days out in hospital. The boss told her, 'I'll let you take vacation days.' She was supposed to get sick days [required in New York City]. When she came out, the hospital told her she had to take care of herself. She tried to work, but she fell down. She had to have a lung operation and she was out two months without working. She never got any sick days. She had worked at our nail salon for six years! When she finally went back to work, the boss told her she could only work certain hours. I knew she was in a lot of pain. We sit in uncomfortable positions all day—after surgery, it was even more painful for her."

Yenelia, like nearly everyone in the group, is undocumented, having crossed the border to find a job to support her family back home in Honduras. Among other things, that has meant that the customer is always right, no matter what. "There was a customer who was unhappy with the job I did, and she wanted to hit me. I got up from my table, and then she threw everything on my table instead—all the chemicals, everything. Another time, a customer came in, and her regular nail technician wasn't there, so she begged me to do her nails for her instead. She didn't like how I did it, and she got really mad and said she wouldn't pay me. I told her that if she wanted the design on her nails, she had to pay for it. But I was recently pregnant, and she wanted to push me, so I had to be careful."

"Another girl didn't like how the color looked on her nails, so she said, 'Give me back my money.' I told her I couldn't—that it wasn't my money. She left and came back with a big group to intimidate me. There's no one to defend you in a situation like that. So I waited for an extra hour after work because I was worried they were waiting outside for me. I was scared—the area is dark, with drug addicts. You're always scared—just because she didn't like the color. It's stressful."

One of Yenelia's fellow workers explains—"At the end of the day, the clients are always right. I don't want to fight, because I always think of my kids. The boss always sides with the clients."

One of the biggest reasons Yenelia and her fellow workers will not fight for their rights is their immigration status. Almost all of them crossed the border without documents in search of jobs to feed their families. When asked if she's working toward some kind of processing of her immigration status, she explains, "There is no process. I don't do anything so they won't find me. I try to avoid public places. I live in fear. If there's a problem I will never call the police."

Customers at Yenelia's nail salon threaten her because of her status. "Customers who get annoyed always say, 'I'm going to call immigration.' So there's a fear that immigration can come at any time. Every day with the news, they're putting down the immigrants. They stereotype you—if you're Hispanic, you're illegal. They try to attack you. If a customer wants to fight, I better exit. If there's punching, they'll call police and then immigration. So that means on the job, they can yell at you, they can put you down."

*   *   *

Avoiding public places means Yenelia mostly just goes to work, to her house, and to her kids' school. The only exception is Workers United. "If the association has a march, I'll go, because I feel supported by the group. But if I have to go anywhere by myself, there's always a fear of deportation. With the group I feel support. Even then, I'm afraid of speaking up in public places. People always say, 'You're not afraid to go speak publicly?' I say, 'No, I'm not doing anything wrong.' But yes, I'm afraid. I'm meeting with legislators, councilmembers, and there's always the fear of being fired, deported. I'm not doing anything wrong. But yes it's fearful."

One of Yenelia's fellow workers, a nail salon worker from Mexico, does not think the fear will ever go away. "The fear will always be there, but you can't let it consume you. You have to keep going. You have to try to have a normal life. I know this isn't my country. I'm here for a long time, I have a stable job, I have to sustain my children. We don't live in luxury, but at least we have a roof and plate of food. You can't go out. You're not in your country. You're in a place that's not yours. It's not your town, your ranch, you're not free. You don't have liberty."

"If I have to go," she continued, "my children have to go with me. But I think about them—how I feel about being here, that's how they will feel about being there [in Mexico]. They go there on summer vacations and stay with my mom, and they tell me they don't want to live there. I tell them, 'How you feel there, is how I feel here. Here I'm a slave to the job, to the bills. You don't have your own life, you don't have a social life. Here it's just work, job, children, seven days of the week. There are no days off. . . . We aren't in our place. We don't feel liberty, tranquility; we feel fear and frustration. You can't live like this. You always have stress, you're biting your nails, thinking what will happen tomorrow. It's impossible to live here."

When asked about their hopes and dreams for the future, some of the women talk about their hopes for their children. One woman says she hopes for "a different country, one without fear, with equality, where everyone has the same rights, no differences, and everyone is respected."

But Yenelia's hopes for the future are different. "I want to go home to my country. Not to stay—I want to see my people, my son. I wouldn't be able to stay because there are no jobs. That's always the dilemma—what can I do? At least here I can send money so they can resolve the problems. But there isn't security here. You live day to day, hope that nothing happens. Hope that they won't put even stricter laws— that I can't work or live. They could make it harder for us to get a place. I'd love to go to my country. Maybe one day I'll go and stay there. My children like it there. I live near the sea—just one block to the sea. We all feel at liberty. They ask me, 'Why don't we live there?' I tell them, 'If we go there, I can't buy you what I buy you here.' It's very hard."

In the meantime, though, Yenelia and her fellow workers feel empowered through Workers United. "I've learned
so much. They've involved us in something positive. With
the little time off I have, I have to give to the Committee
to support and learn a little. I have four kids—I have to take
them to school, to the doctor, I have to cook, wash. But I
take a little time to go to the meetings on my day off—it's
important." One of her fellow workers explains the impact:
"They've taught me a lot. We didn't know our rights. Now
we learned it all, we can demand something. Demand our
rights. Demand time to eat lunch. It's not the same as before.
Before when they said you have to hurry I had lots of fear,
thinking, 'They're going to fire me.' I learn each time more,
I feel more empowered to talk to the boss, tell them my
rights. I'm able to tell other coworkers to not be afraid. It has
helped me. I've grown a lot."

6

Debbie and Marshan

Working While Incarcerated

"It's literally slave labor"

Debbie Leggio was born and raised on Long Island, New York. Her father was fourth-generation Irish American, and her mother was third-generation Norwegian. They met through the military—Debbie's father was an Army captain, and her mother was a USO dancer. They met at an Army dance and ended up having six children together. Debbie was the youngest.

Debbie's father was an alcoholic and died when she was nine years old, and her grandmother passed six months later. Her oldest sister, who had been living with her grandmother, was recuperating from a terrible car accident that left her permanently disabled. For most of Debbie's childhood, her immediate family consisted of Debbie, her mother, and her much older sister.

The three women survived off her father's social security and veteran's benefits and a small life insurance policy that did not last. Despite these challenges, Debbie thrived in school. "I enjoyed school. I did very well in high school—I was in all the extracurricular activities. I was captain of the kick line [the dance team], I was in all the musicals, I played volleyball." Debbie got accepted into a college in Pennsylvania but had to come back to New York after just one semester. "We had lost our house. I had to come back to help get everything situated, help us move into an apartment. I went to the community college and started working." While in high school, Debbie had been working at a local deli owned by her sister's friend. When she came back from Pennsylvania, she returned to the deli to keep working. She met the deli owner's nephew at the deli and ended up marrying him. "We will have been married thirty-three years this year."

Some years later, Debbie found work as a bookkeeper, and then a comptroller, and ultimately settled at a nonprofit organization in Long Island for many years managing their accounts. Over a period of eight years, from 2001 to 2009, Debbie moved her way up in the organization from staff accountant to director of finance.

In 2009, Debbie's husband got a job with a private company doing air traffic controlling in California. With their son now grown up and gone to college, Debbie and her husband moved to Tracy, in Northern California, and Debbie once again started working in finance for a nonprofit in San Francisco.

It was at this time that Debbie received a phone call from the district attorney back in Long Island; the state was pursuing Debbie's conviction for embezzling funds while working at the nonprofit in Long Island. The executive director of the nonprofit had been engaged in some inappropriate activity—hiring family members, falsifying board minutes, inflating her salary, and failing to oversee the finances. When the executive director was terminated, a forensic audit was conducted that revealed Debbie's actions as well. "I was charged with grand larceny. I had been in a bad situation and made poor choices. I take full responsibility for my actions. I went through years of therapy. I had what they called adult child of alcoholic syndrome, with addictive behavior that comes out as an adult. . . . There was no oversight and I got caught up."

Still in California, Debbie obtained a lawyer and fought her case for two years, before finally being offered a deal—they would drop larger charges if she pled guilty. "I had been fighting it from 2010 to 2013, and I needed it to be over." Attorneys' fees had cost Debbie a lot of money. "I don't know how I survived—I didn't know what was going to happen. It was just awful." Debbie was working full-time in California, and the executive director of the nonprofit in New York was sending lawyers to speak to Debbie's new employers in California as well. In the end, Debbie was sentenced for two and a third to seven years in prison, and Debbie flew to New York to serve her sentence.

"I started out at Bedford Hills Maximum Security Prison for an orientation. If you have a longer sentence or a more violent crime, you'd stay there. Otherwise you'd be sent elsewhere." In Debbie's case, she was sent to the Albion Correctional Facility in Buffalo/Rochester, six hours north of New York City. At first they put Debbie in a GED class, though she had completed high school and gone to college. "You have to verify that I graduated from high school—so they stuck me in GED class until they could verify my education. I kept telling them I was taking the place of someone who really needed their GED."

Once she completed the GED verification, Debbie was allowed to work in the prison. "I became a porter—cleaning the bathroom and showers, mopping the floors, cleaning the rooms. The rooms were set up like army barracks, with bunk beds, a common area, bathroom, and showers. I was paid 16 cents an hour. Since I didn't have any other programming to be a part of—no drug counseling or alcohol counseling—I ended up working six hours a day, six days a week." After some time, Debbie was fortune enough to receive a "promotion." "I was chosen to be an IPA—an inmate program associate. I was lucky enough to get that. I became a teaching assistant in a general business vocational program, teaching two modules six hours away. I got a raise to 25 cents per hour. That was the most you could make as an IPA."

Debbie went on to work other jobs in prison—as a peer counselor, for example, in the transitional services department. "I would help women with reentry for 25 cents an hour. I'd help them find housing, help them with their resumes, conduct job searches for them." There were other jobs—some people worked for a private organization that hired incarcerated women to conduct HIV awareness education with their peers for 16 to 25 cents an hour.

But the most exploitative job situation was the women working for Corcraft, a private manufacturing company that located its factories on the grounds of Albion Correctional Facility, the women's prison where Debbie was held. "Corcraft workers made lockers, garbage cans, and other metal objects. The women were doing welding and painting— jobs that would be unionized manufacturing jobs on the outside." The company argued that they were training the women for union jobs when they got out, but no one was ever able to get those jobs when they got out. "Let them try to become part of the union as a convicted felon. How are they supposed to get a job? They knew the girls didn't have a choice. They're making a fortune off these women." Corcraft has factories in all fourteen women's prisons across the state of New York.

There were other jobs as well. Many women were working in the mess halls for 16 cents an hour; "they were supposedly teaching them food service." And, of course, the state also profits off prison labor. "Whenever you call the DMV in New York State, it's inmates answering the phone." And outdoor jobs. "I fought to get outside clearance. I finally got it. I worked on the outside grounds crew—landscaping, doing outdoor work." And then a terrible accident happened. "A couple of weeks into it, I was moving tree limbs and I tripped and fell and broke my wrist. Usually you'd get workers' compensation for something like that. Instead they handcuffed and shackled me—with my broken wrist and my bone moved out of place." The guards took Debbie handcuffed, shackled, and in excruciating pain on a long walk to the prison infirmary. Doctors confirmed her wrist was broken and had to insert a metal plate and screws inside her to fix it.

After that, Debbie could no longer work outside the facility, and working was essential. "The money you earn in prison goes into your account—that's what you use to buy the things you need for your personal hygiene at the prison commissary." The prison did not provide adequate necessities—shampoo, toothpaste, toilet paper, tampons, sanitary napkins, deodorant—and so the women were often forced to use their meager earnings to obtain very basic necessities. "The toilet paper would run out, and if you don't have the money to buy it at the commissary, you're out of luck. There was always a shortage of sanitary napkins, so you'd have to buy them. People who couldn't afford it were given toothpaste with lye that they use to whiten shoes and socks—those people's teeth were falling out."

After two years, Debbie was able to appeal to obtain work release, in which she could work several days a week and report back to the prison on other days. She was able to obtain a job at a bagel café on Long Island. But even at that point, her income was garnished. "All my money went into an inmate account, and they took 20 percent of it. You had to ask for money for your personal needs, even to get a MetroCard." But even when properly asked, the money was not forthcoming. "More than one time, when I got a check for a MetroCard, it bounced. I was not allowed to have a bank account—we had to use check-cashing facilities for the checks we requested." Debbie was also not allowed to have a driver's license or social security card, so she could not drive and was reliant on mass transit.

While on work release, Debbie had the good fortune to meet Rita Zimmer, the executive director of HousingPlus, a nonprofit organization serving homeless women, women veterans, and low-income women with children. Debbie had been volunteering with a group doing business planning for women and went to do a presentation to a group of tenants; Rita happened to be there. "Rita heard my story and gave me a job while I was on work release. I became the coordinator of learning and development and was in charge of piloting a life skills program with the women." Even with this job, however, the prison took all of her income, kept 20 percent of it, and then issued checks for her personal necessities.

Debbie was finally released, able to move back to California and rejoin her family. She did not work for a year as she was getting reacclimated into society. She finally found a job as the operations manager at the Ella Baker Center for Human Rights, which works to end mass incarceration. After being incarcerated herself, Debbie felt it would be good to work for others in the same situation, and to speak out against the prison labor system.

In fact, the ability for prisons and private companies to hire incarcerated people and pay them nothing is based on the exception to the Thirteenth Amendment, which ended slavery but which allows for slavery in the context of incarceration. "It's literally slave labor," says Debbie. "People don't know about criminal justice. They think it's about retribution. But the labor that inmates do is crazy for the amount of money they receive. They're expected to survive on pennies. The commissary prices are not low—they're not adjusted for the circumstances. So you're spending all your money."

In county-level prisons, inmates are also expected to use their earnings to be able to make phone calls to loved ones, which are priced much higher than phone calls on the outside.

"It's ridiculous. You're making money off of inmates. People say you're paying your debt to society, but what are the limitations of that? Keeping people incarcerated for years is not the answer. You're spending more money doing that and not solving the problem. I was working—I was a productive member of society. I should have been paid." Debbie recognizes her privilege—as a white woman, with a supportive family on the outside who was able to send her things, and not having the worst experiences with prison guards. "It could have been a lot worse. Bedford was horrible. It all depends on the officers. There were instances where they lost it and started to choke an inmate. It's unnerving. They're further traumatizing people who are already traumatized."

Marshan was born and raised in the southeast side of Chicago. His father was a bus and truck driver, and his mother worked at the Thunderbird car manufacturing plant. As a young child, Marshan remembers his father taking him and his brother to work, first as a bus driver for Trailways bus lines, then as a truck driver delivering meat products to restaurants, and even as a school bus driver at one point, dropping kids off at school. With both parents working, Marshan and his family lived in an apartment in a residential neighborhood in the South Side of Chicago.

Marshan's parents later divorced, and his mother took the kids to move into his grandmother's house. "My grandma's neighborhood was rougher. My mom's brothers lived there and were in gangs, selling drugs. I wasn't aware of it until later years, until high school." As he grew older, Marshan became aware that his parents had been selling drugs as well. "They couldn't make ends meet, couldn't find jobs to pay enough, so they were selling drugs to supplement their income. My dad was driving a school bus earlier, but later, working on and off, he couldn't find jobs. He did have

trouble finding jobs, or he'd work temp jobs, and then be laid off. In the end they decided [selling drugs] was a better use of their time than earning a minimum wage."

One of Marshan's uncles moved in with his grandmother in middle school; he sold drugs as well. "I felt a level of pride—he was well known. People knew who we were and didn't mess with us. At the time, we really stuck together. We were a close-knit family. Grandma's house was a head-quarters for the kids—everyone always wanted to be there because something was always happening. It was a source of pride—I was happy that I had my family, and we were together."

When Marshan's brother James graduated from eighth grade and started high school, he moved in with his grandmother and uncles. The uncles introduced James to their business, and James starting working for them, selling drugs. This led to Marshan's involvement. "The summer before high school, my brother introduced me to his drug business, and I started selling for him. It was small amounts initially, increasing as his business grew. I was fourteen at the time. It was 1990—we were selling both powder cocaine and crack cocaine, and getting it from connections in the neighborhood. One of our uncle's friends was like an uncle to us—we'd get it from him. He was a big drug dealer."

At some point the drug selling business became dangerous for fourteen-year-old Marshan. "I was out waiting for my friend, standing with him while he was robbed at gunpoint. My brother had been robbed twice. In 1992, my brother got robbed again, by people coming to buy a large amount of drugs. They took his drugs and money and kidnapped me, had me drop them where I'd picked them up at, and then let me go."

Marshan's brother tried to reason with the people who stole his drugs and money, but they would not listen. "My brother asked me to steal a car to travel to where the drugs and money were being held." James's friends then took the car to get the drugs and money back, and killed two people in the process.

Marshan and his brother were away, visiting family in Detroit, when the murders happened. They had been threat-

ened by gang members in the neighborhood and had been
encouraged by their mother to go visit family in Detroit.
When they returned, two weeks later, Marshan alone was
arrested.

"The police had learned about the robbery. My brother
went to talk to the police, hoping to tell them he had nothing
to do with the murders. Then they came and interviewed
me, took my statement, and denied me any opportunity to
talk to my mother, brother, or a lawyer. They interviewed
me by myself; I was sixteen years old. My brother was never
arrested—I was trying to protect him. I didn't tell them he
had asked me to steal the car." In the end, neither Marshan's
brother James nor the two friends who were involved in the
killing ended up imprisoned—only Marshan. "They didn't
have enough evidence to arrest my brother. Of the other
two friends, one got life parole, and the other was let free—
they didn't have enough evidence to try him."

Although Marshan was the youngest and least involved person in the incident, the police arrested him based on the
charge that he "aided and abetted with an illegal act, which
was a felony murder," though he was not involved in the
murder of either of the two people killed. And in Illinois,
individuals convicted of more than one murder receive a
mandatory life sentence without parole, regardless of your
age or level of participation. This was the charge leveled
at sixteen-year-old Marshan. Marshan believed that the

police were punishing him in some ways for refusing to testify against his brother. "They tried to get me to make my brother pay for it. They tried to pressure me to testify against my co-defendants, and I wouldn't do it."

Marshan's first trial in 1993 resulted in a hung jury. "One of the jurors refused to hold me guilty, because they thought it was unfair." The judge declared a mistrial. In June 1994, Marshan was retried and ultimately convicted. "The judge told me that if he had discretion, he would not order a mandatory life sentence, given that I was under the influence of my older brother." The judge called Marshan a "bright lad" based on his testimony at trial, letters that he had written to the judge, and the fact that Marshan had earned his GED during the two years he was awaiting trial. His social workers had presented a report about Marshan's behavior, school records, and potential for rehabilitation. But in the end, "the judge said his hands were tied, because of Illinois policy requiring a mandatory life sentence for those found guilty of more than one murder. My lawyer had told me that if I was found guilty, this would be the only sentence available to the judge because I was a juvenile. If I had been an adult, the judge could have given me a life sentence or the death penalty."

At the age of eighteen, Marshan found himself with a life of prison ahead of him. "I was in denial. I didn't think I'd get life without parole. I didn't hurt anyone, kill anyone, didn't even have a weapon. In my mind, I didn't understand the mandatory nature of it. I didn't understand until the judge said that. When I realized he wanted to give me a lesser sentence, that really broke my heart. I was crying like a baby in the courtroom, even before he said it."

While awaiting trial, Marshan had been held at the Cook County Juvenile Center and the Cook County Jail. After he was sentenced in 1994, he was sent to the Pontiac Correctional Center, an adult prison. "It was crazy—my first time in adult prison. It was totally a shock. . . . I was terrified—I didn't know what to expect. I was eighteen years old. I didn't know anyone—who to trust, who was a friend or foe. There was danger—fights, people getting stabbed, people getting shot by officers, lots of gunshots going off."

It was in this violent environment that Marshan began working for a subminimum wage while in prison. "My first job was as a janitor in the healthcare unit. We earned $30 a month, and after ninety days, that went up to $45 per month."

Most people in Pontiac worked in the kitchen, also starting at $30 per month. Everyone worked eight hours per day, six and sometimes seven days per week. "You technically didn't have a day off. You could request a day off, but typically you'd have to work with no days off." Subminimum wage pay in prison might be somewhat more acceptable if it were voluntary, but Marshan explained that in reality it was not. Although it was not mandatory to have a job while in prison, the institution could discipline inmates for refusing a job assignment. "They drafted me to work in the kitchen, but I didn't want to work in the kitchen. I had no desire to work in the kitchen; I was going to school. I didn't want to miss a class offering, but they drafted me to come work in the kitchen. I didn't want the job, but I had to work it."

Marshan was trying to earn a certificate in business management while in prison. He was trying to get a college degree. "They only offered certain classes at a time— sometimes they were classes that I had already taken, sometimes they had no class offerings I needed."

While trying to get his degree Marshan worked multiple jobs, as a cellhouse worker, laundry porter, and midnight kitchen staff, all for the paltry sum of $30 per month for eight hours of work per day, six to seven days per week. This meant Marshan and his fellow inmates were earning, on average, 13 cents per hour. "The prison system was saving money by having inmates do these jobs rather than unionized safety and sanitation workers," he said.

The other job options for people in prison, outside of working directly for the prison, were controlled by Illinois Correctional Industries (ICI), a quasi-public for-profit entity that hired incarcerated people to manufacture clothing, furniture like desks and bookshelves, and commissary items like bar soap for other Illinois government agencies. Marshan ended up working in an ICI meat processing plant; ICI also ran a bakery producing bread and cookies. ICI jobs would pay more than other prison jobs, up to $200 a month, or about 85 cents per hour.

Marshan and his fellow workers did not accept these meager wages without complaint. "We would ask for raises—everyone complained about it. The amount we were paid was set in the 1970s, and there had never been any increase." But, of course, like other workers, many incarcerated workers at Pontiac feared speaking up about the wages because they were worried about losing their job, being disciplined or transferred, or facing other retaliatory actions. "I was fired for complaining about a job. When I was working in the meat processing plant, sometimes some meat would be missing. If the supervisor didn't know who did it, we would all be charged double; they'd deduct it from all our paychecks even though they knew we weren't involved. I complained—told them the policy was unfair, and that it wouldn't deter people from stealing since everyone would end up paying for the missing meat rather than just the one person. The supervisor got upset with me and fired me. Once you get a disciplinary report, you have to wait until you can apply for another job. . . . Sometimes it takes a while—supervisors will talk to other supervisors and tell them not to hire you."

Marshan's paltry earnings would be deposited into a "trust fund" account that he could spend on commissary products or send to his family. But there would always be a deduction from his earnings to reimburse the state for the cost of his incarceration. And commissary products were both essential and costly. "The state didn't give us soap or

deodorant. . . . You had to buy these items in the commissary." Inmates who did not have funds from their family
or from work were given $9 per month to buy items in
the commissary. While the monthly amount given had not
increased since the 1970s, the price of commissary goods
increased each year based on federal price increases, which
meant you were able to buy less and less each year. Marshan reports that goods were more expensive in the prison
commissary than outside. "You could buy a ramen noodles
packet for $1—you could get ten of the same for $1 outside.
A bar of soap cost $1, and toothpaste cost $2. You were
given one toilet paper roll a week, but it didn't last, and you
needed more—and that cost $1 to $2."

During his time in prison, Marshan had been working to
reduce his sentence through "good behavior." This opportunity to reduce his sentence was not available to Marshan initially, but while in prison, this became a possibility. Illinois
prison policy allowed for sentences to be reduced by one day
for every day of "good behavior." In this way, Marshan was
working to reduce his sentence slowly from a life sentence
to half of his life. But this is where work assignments, never
up to the discretion of the worker, had the cost of freedom
attached to them. "The prison could also take 'good time'
from you. They could issue a disciplinary report if you don't
come to work. You can get disciplined for not taking a work
assignment, not showing up. If you disobey a direct order
to take a work assignment, your good time can be taken

away. Even your work supervisor can take time away." This policy gives work supervisors inside prison—both those in the prison and those in ICI—complete authority over their staff. Incarcerated workers had little discretion about which jobs to work or the conditions of work.

In 2012, the U.S. Supreme Court ruled in *Miller v. Alabama* that it was unconstitutional to give juveniles a life sentence without parole. This forced a judge to reconsider Marshan's sentence; he was resentenced to a term of years that he had already served, and let free in 2016. After almost twenty years of work in prison, Marshan left prison having saved $500. He found work first as a real estate appraisal analyst, and then as a Starbucks supervisor, until he finally found his calling working as a project manager at Restore Justice, a nonprofit working on criminal justice reform.

When asked about the argument that prisoners need not be paid a full minimum wage for work performed inside because they owe a debt to society, Marshan dissents. "Our debt to society is paid by our freedom being taken away. We weren't sentenced to hard labor or to work for free. We were sentenced to be separated from society. It would be useful and productive for society if they did pay people inside a fair minimum wage and allowed them to save. It would take pressure off our families who are working [on the outside] and have to pay their bills so we can make phone calls and have soap. We should be able to take responsibility for our lives and save for our eventual release. If they didn't have us to do [the work], they'd have to pay someone to do it and pay more."

ICI and other for-profit entities hiring inmates argue that they should be allowed to pay paltry wages because they are providing inmates with skills to be used on the outside. Marshan responds, "We're getting skills, but we're working. They're getting more benefit from us than we're getting from our pay. It's not a good excuse for them not to pay a fair minimum wage or give a valid reason. People on the outside get skills, but they get paid." The only real difference, then, between the meat processing worker in the prison and a meat processing worker on the outside is the value placed on the incarcerated person's worth. This should give pause given the overwhelming overrepresentation of Black and brown men and women incarcerated in Illinois and across the country, often at very young ages like Marshan.

7

Vianne

Delivery Workers Seek Respect

"You are not going to talk to me like this"

Vianne Curiel had wanted to be a singer songwriter for as long she could remember. Music was her passion. "I've been writing songs since I was thirteen!" she recalls. She spent her earliest years across the U.S.-Mexico border in San Luis Río Colorado before her parents moved to Yuma, Arizona. "I was a baby. My parents and I lived in an old trailer in Sonora until I was two or three, then they came back to Arizona and they bought a house. My dad was a field worker, and my mom worked for the DMV. From there they slowly saved until they could establish their own car dealership."

Vianne had dual citizenship and went to Mexico to study communications and marketing at the Universidad Regiomontana in Monterrey. By the time she returned in 2012, she felt that as "an independent artist, I didn't have funds to pursue my music career." Her parents weren't in a position to help her financially. In any case, they didn't approve of her musical efforts and wanted her to follow in their footsteps and work in the car dealership. "They kicked me out of the house," she said. "They left me out on the streets. I didn't know what to do. So I moved to LA with $200." Vianne always said that she was going to live in LA, but she never thought it would happen like that. She packed her car with the few belongings she had and moved into a studio apartment with her cousin. "She said you have a month to get a job and pay rent."

Finding a good job in LA proved very difficult. "I started building up my resume, but I couldn't find a job," she said. Part of the problem was that her work experience was all in Mexico. Vianne was doing everything she could to survive in Los Angeles. She explained, "I was always tight on money because I wouldn't make enough, even working four or five jobs. It was very exhausting." Vianne applied to work as a food delivery worker for Postmates and DoorDash, two relatively recent app-based delivery services. Vianne credits this decision with helping get her back on her feet. "I heard about Postmates from someone I knew in LA, and they said this is easy, quick money." She found the idea embarrassing at first, but decided she would just go ahead and try it. Embarrassed by her own embarrassment, she thought, "Seriously, I have to become a better human."

After Vianne filled out the applications for Postmates and DoorDash and underwent a brief training session, "I just got in my car and I started delivering food." As with most gig economy workers, Vianne continued working multiple jobs. "I was working at Postmates, and I was working for a gym as well. I was working for the gym membership because I couldn't afford a gym. And then I worked for a meal prepping company where I cooked meal prep for athletes and washed dishes." Unfortunately, this led her to put her true love, her music career, on hiatus. "I stopped making music for that whole year and got very depressed about it. I didn't have inspiration or motivation to write songs anymore because I was trying to get back on my feet." She sees 2017 as a make-or-break experience, "one of the worst years of my life. It was a turning point: either life would break me or there would be a breakthrough and I'd just start all over, start fresh." Vianne recalled being told that if you make it a year in LA, everything gets easier, adding, "LA is a very expensive city to live in. I can tell you that for sure."

The history of delivery service is tied to the flow of population, spurred in turn by industrialization. Just as economic demand—the combination of economic opportunity elsewhere and economic hardship at home—draws people from around the world to major trade centers in the United States, Europe, and Asia, so it drew people from their farms and country villages to urban centers. As people lost or gave up their livestock, milk would be delivered in metal barrels by entrepreneurial dairy farmers. As the industry consolidated, daily home deliveries in glass bottles became the norm. And then the advent of refrigeration and the emergence of suburbia slowly whittled away the market share for the home delivery of basic food products.

Takeout food has always been a hallmark of transit hubs, serving hungry travelers and laborers on their way to work. But it also has a secret history tied to emancipation. Black women found they could make a living selling hot meals to passersby, and individuals could order food for carryout even if they weren't allowed to dine in segregated restaurants.

The delivery of food picked up in the 1920s with the advent of Chinese restaurants opened by immigrants in California. What was previously known as an "oyster pail" to carry steamed bivalves became the ubiquitous Chinese takeout box. In the 1950s, with the growth of suburbia, restaurants began offering "TV dinners" to be enjoyed at home in front of the TV. Pizza quickly became the primary food delivery item, leading to delivery wars with pizza chains expanding on the promise of "thirty minutes or it's free."

The restaurant industry created the logistics infrastructure necessary to deliver food: menus were slipped underneath doors, people called establishments to place an order, and delivery workers were employees of the restaurants. While many restaurants offered delivery services, and many more offered takeout, it was only the recent advent of the app delivery platform that opened up delivery across the country, covering every known concept and segment, from McDonald's to Michelin-starred restaurants. The restaurant industry projected $863 billion in sales in 2019, with

$107 billion, or over 12 percent of that revenue, from online food delivery. Direct app platform–to–consumer food delivery accounts for over 50 percent of that $107 billion.[1]

Prior to the arrival of companies like Seamless, Door-Dash, and Postmates, you might call a restaurant directly, order food over the phone, and wait for a delivery worker who worked directly for the restaurant to bring you food. Of course, not all restaurants could afford delivery staff, and not all restaurants delivered. The convenience of being able to have any food of your desire brought to your doorstep is the selling point of these proliferating delivery network companies. Now all the customer has to do is open an app on their phone or their computer and make an order with the expectation that it will arrive relatively quickly. In the case of DoorDash and Postmates, the app then sends out a call to an army of independently contracted delivery workers. The First World desire for convenience thus provides precarious jobs for immigrants from the Third World, cuts into the revenue of millions of small business restaurants nationwide, and produces profits for large tech companies.

These app platforms are a major component of what is known as the gig economy. Over fifteen million workers around the country work in nonstandard work arrangements, as independent contractors, temporary workers, and on-call workers—and their numbers are growing. More than a million and a half of these are new gig workers who provide services mediated by an app or online platform.[2]

Food delivery is now one of the two largest categories of gig work, along with ride-share apps. Well-known companies such as Grubhub, Postmates, Uber, Lyft, and TaskRabbit have upended the traditional worker classification system that provided worker protections in the "old economy." Food delivery drivers have transitioned from being restaurant employees to independent contractors, entrenching delivery as a subminimum wage occupation while simultaneously eroding legal protections extended to workers.

The growth of the delivery market has also had implications for tipped workers within restaurants. Tipped workers, including servers, have to take and enter orders, pack and bag deliveries, and pass them off to delivery workers. These tasks are conducted while earning a subminimum wage, and take away from an in-store subminimum wage worker's potential to earn tips. Employers are required to report a minimum of 8 percent of an employee's gross sales as tips, and workers are at times required to include these delivery orders in their gross sales, meaning that they are liable for taxes on tips that they never receive.[3]

While delivery has the potential to add a revenue stream to a restaurant, delivery platforms also create an added pressure on restaurant owners. When using a delivery platform, owners have to pay a fee per order to the platforms, reducing their profit margins and leading to greater pressure on staff.[4] Companies like Uber Eats charge restaurants 30 percent of the bill, and DoorDash charges a commission per order and an advertising commission—a payment for advertising their restaurant on their app.

As gig platforms have taken over the food delivery and ride-share markets, unions and worker advocates have sought to ensure gig workers like Vianne at least the same protections enjoyed by other workers—and to push back on multibillion-dollar corporations' desire to maintain these workers as independent contractors exempt from minimum wage, unemployment insurance benefits—which became a major issue during the pandemic—and other benefits and protections guaranteed other workers in their states. While the companies attempted to posit that these work arrangements created more flexibility for drivers and were an innovative evolution of work, in fact corporations' attempts to label workers as independent contractors dates back to the New Deal, when companies sought to misclassify first Black workers and then other workers as independent contractors to similarly avoid minimum wage and other protections awarded employees—a trend so common even before the emergence of gig companies it has been labeled "misclassification."

In part since so many of the newly expanding gig companies were born in Silicon Valley, California, much of the worker organizing efforts to fight misclassification and establish greater protection for gig workers started in California. In 2018, the efforts of unions and worker organizations led to the Supreme Court of California issuing a landmark decision in the case *Dynamex Operations West, Inc. v. Superior Court.* Dynamex stated that most workers are employees and that any company seeking to classify a worker as an independent contractor must meet a stringent burden of proof to do so.

In early 2019 these efforts gained steam with a series of *New York Times* exposés on food delivery companies such as DoorDash. Among all the harassment, safety, and compensation issues lifted up by these exposés, the one that stirred the most consumer outrage was that several of these companies were deducting the delivery workers' payments by the amount they were tipped. In fact, these companies were simply emulating the restaurant industry's subminimum wage system dating back to Emancipation—reducing their workers' pay based on how much they were tipped. While there has been some debate among worker organizers of gig workers as to whether they should fight to eliminate independent contractor status for these workers completely, there is no debate with regard to whether these workers deserve a full, livable wage with tips on top and all of the rights and benefits that other workers are afforded by their state. Clearly, as long as we allow any industry to use a subminimum wage because of tips, more and more industries will seek to follow suit.

In September 2019, the California State Legislature expanded upon the *Dynamex* decision with the passage of Assembly Bill 5 (AB5), which required gig platform companies to treat their workers as employees, with all the rights and protections awarded other employees in the state of California, including minimum wage, paid sick leave, workers' compensation, and other rights. The bill was hailed as a national model for instituting workers' rights in the gig sector, but the gig platforms immediately pushed back, mobilizing hundreds of millions of dollars to put into Proposition 22, a ballot measure placed on the November 2020 ballot that would not only repeal AB5 but also allow the gig platforms to pay their workers the equivalent of a subminimum wage. The gig companies united behind this ballot measure and launched a public relations campaign to attempt to portray that independent contractor status was necessary to ensure workers' flexibility—and thus a feature all workers preferred—and also that their measure was backed by progressive and racial justice organizations. Despite the fact that the pandemic put all of these workers in grave danger while they were offered none of the unemployment insurance benefits given other workers, the gig companies were able to use expensive and sophisticated propaganda to confuse voters. The companies sent out mailers purporting to be progressive voter guides called "Feel the Bern, Progressive Voter Guide," "Council of Concerned Women Voters Guide," and "Our Voice, Latino Voter Guide"—none of which are actual organizations—that provided guidance on a number of other progressive ballot measures and a "yes" on Proposition 22. These mailers suggested that U.S. senator Bernie

Sanders and progressive women's and Latinx community groups supported these companies' attempt to exempt
themselves from basic worker protections. The expensive
propaganda worked, and Proposition 22 passed overwhelm-
ingly. As a result, until laws pass to overturn Proposition
22, gig workers in California and all states nationwide are
subminimum wage workers.

The California fight continues, and unions and worker
advocates in other states such as New York and Illinois are
now attempting to learn from the California experience to
organize and create rights for gig workers. However, these
states have an additional barrier that California did not
have: a subminimum wage for tipped workers. Even if these
states—or any of the forty-three states with a subminimum
wage for tipped workers—succeeded in passing a bill such
as AB5, guaranteeing gig workers the same protections and
rights as other tipped workers in their state, they would be
paid a subminimum wage since they are tipped workers. It
is thus essential to unify these efforts for One Fair Wage—a
full minimum wage with tips on top for all workers, including restaurant workers, gig workers, and all of the other sectors currently receiving a subminimum wage—as well as
unemployment insurance benefits, earned paid sick leave,
paid family leave, and all other rights and benefits.

Vianne recalled using DoorDash first. She received training in the app, and also received a Visa card to pay for food
if customers hadn't already paid. "You just get in your car,

you turn on your app, and it gives you a delivery," Vianne explained, "and you just accept 'yes.' And that's how you start delivering." After joining DoorDash, Vianne joined Postmates right away. "I [joined] both of them to see which was better," she said.

She preferred Postmates. "I felt like I got my money's worth. I used Postmates more because Postmates has better pay and it's more lenient. I'm sure Postmates can improve on their pay, but I was making a lot more money." Vianne explained that at Postmates, she was able to receive all of her tips. "People would always leave tips. It was very rare for people to not leave a tip. Sometimes, they would give me $2 or $3, but they would give me something. Sometimes, people would tip me up to $150 or $250, you know, it was amazing. She recalls one customer's large order. "He ordered these big packages of meat, and it was heavy, and I was upset because it was heavy. 'He better tip me,' I remember thinking, because this is hard-core. When I got there, the guy was super, super nice. He actually got the box for me. And the next day I saw the tip. It was an $85 tip. I think what [people] do sometimes is tip like they do at a restaurant based on the total amount of what they spend on the food. So I think that's what the guy did, because I think his meat was, like, $400. It was expensive meat. I think he tipped me like 25 or 30 percent."

At DoorDash, on the other hand, "it felt like I had a set pay for each delivery." DoorDash is one of a handful of companies that have publicly defended and received public criticism for their policy of discounting tips from workers' pay. For example, Vianne explained, "DoorDash might offer a higher $12 delivery fee per order. Let's say they tip me $15 or $20 on top of [that]. I'm never going to see the tip because DoorDash just gives me $12." Since all platform workers are classified as independent contractors, they aren't covered by the guarantees that tips belong to employees, as was recently added to the Fair Labor Standards Act. Vianne added, "That's why I would pick Postmates instead of DoorDash. Because Postmates would do that, the rate plus whatever the person gave you in tips." In 2019, the CEO of Postmates publicly announced his support for One Fair Wage and the company's commitment to ensure that tips would not be discounted against worker payments.

Vianne was shocked by DoorDash's 2019 announcement that it would continue to discount tips from the delivery payment, a policy it has reversed and then reinstated multiple times. "People are not gonna want that. This should be a platform that's win-win. This is a win-win situation when you pay people right. When you get paid well, you even do the work with pride." She remembers her initial feeling of embarrassment. "I had to learn, and I had to grow, and take pride in what I do. So every delivery I would try to do my best, greet people, smile at people, and do my job because I was representing the company that sustained me."

However, despite being able to receive tips on top of a

delivery fee at Postmates, Vianne still faced multiple challenges delivering for both companies. For one thing, the pay was not enough if customers did not tip on top. Vianne once delivered a Starbucks order to one well-known celebrity. Starbucks has changed since mobile ordering, but at the time, "you had to go in, order the drinks, pay, and then you wait for the drinks [to] deliver to the person. I was so upset because he didn't give me a tip. What the hell, dude! Even if it's just one dollar, give something. Don't just not tip."

Customer abuse was also a problem. "I was delivering a big banquet," she recalls. She had to pick up the order from an Italian restaurant in Beverly Hills. "It was a big order. I got there three or four minutes late to pick up the food." The manager, who was white, shouted at her, "Who the hell do you think you are coming so late? This food needs to be in right now. Hurry up! And where's your Postmates bag?" Vianne replied, "The food's not going to fit in the Postmates bag." The manager shouted at her that she didn't care. Vianne told her, "You are not going to talk to me like this. I am doing a delivery, and you have no right to talk to me like this." The manager threw the plates at her. "She was so rude. I felt discriminated against. I think they paid $300 for it. When I got to the customer, and I gave them the food, and they were super nice to me. They tipped me super well and everything."

Vianne described another horrible customer experience. "He was the rudest human being on the planet. I actually cried. I sent him a message because I guess he was pissed because I couldn't find his apartment. I told him, 'I can't find your apartment number, can you come outside and pick up the food for me?' And when he saw me, he said to me, 'You're such a fucking bitch. You can't even get out of your car to give me my food, which I'm paying for.' He just grabs the food from my hand. And I was in total shock. I didn't know how to react. I thought, *I don't need to be doing this stuff.* I just sent him a message, 'God bless your soul.' That's it. I was so pissed. I was so mad."

Beyond tips and customer abuse, delivery work itself is difficult and stressful. Vianne said, "In LA, it is very hard to actually find parking when you deliver food. There's never parking." At times Vianne would get so stressed out that she would cancel an order. "Sometimes it would get so crazy that there weren't even places to park and it was hard. . . . It is easy money to work for this type of company, but it is also a hustle. You have to go pick up the food, and sometimes the food's not even ready. You have to wait, pick up the food, and then go deliver it for someone." The platforms have responded by integrating orders, "so, if you're nearby, you pick up two or three deliveries at the same time."

Parking tickets were particularly frustrating. "I remember I had to park at a meter one day and I put a quarter in the wrong meter and got a ticket. It was like $60 to $70 in Beverly Hills. I remember clearly that day. I was very upset. I thought, *You know what? I'm done.*" The wear and tear on the car was an additional worry. Vianne said to herself, "You are putting miles on your car. You are wasting gas. You are risking your life on a daily basis because living in LA you can get in a car accident. God has been with me along the way, but I think I added forty thousand miles in a year or year and a half."

Vianne was working twelve-hour days, from morning to night, to make ends meet. At most she could do three deliveries an hour, but it was difficult due to the traffic. "Supposedly, you would be making about $20 to $25 an hour, but it was very, very rare. It really depended on how fast you were, how good you were, and if traffic was okay." The platforms would offer weekly bonuses to incentivize deliveries. "If you hit seventy-five or eighty deliveries Postmates would give you $500 [total], but they'd give you four days just to accomplish it. It would take you the whole day, but I did it."

The work was overwhelming at times. "I remember I would deliver food for people and I would see them just lying in their bed or sitting on their couch, doing nothing, just watching TV and ordering food. I remember saying, one day I'm going to have that. I'm going to be able to do that. I'm going to have my own couch, sit on my couch, do nothing, just order food in."

Vianne finally decided to follow her family's lead back into the car business and was hired to work in the internet department at a Hyundai dealership. She quickly started moving sixteen to thirty units a month. She now has a one-bedroom apartment in Koreatown with parking, a rarity in Los Angeles. At first she still worked at Postmates as well because she wasn't making enough money and needed to pay off multiple parking tickets. She left the company just months before it was acquired by Uber—which makes the company's relatively more progressive stances uncertain. She was promoted and is now working on her music again. "I'm doing amazing, and really good things are coming towards me. And now because of these jobs that I got, I said it's time to get back in my music career. In September, I launched my next single, and in December I launched my other one, and I've been going up and trying to get into live sessions and just, you know, going little by little, and that's my story."

The elements of a delivery job that are constant are: "nasty weather, dangerous encounters with cars, and long hours for wages and tips that can fall well below the minimum wage."[5] For restaurant tipped workers, the dependence on tips leads workers to tolerate behaviors they otherwise would not; for delivery workers, the reliance on tips often leads them to work in dangerous conditions. Bicycle-based delivery jobs are among the most dangerous jobs. In Boston, a study of bike delivery workers found that "70 percent had suffered an injury resulting in medical attention or lost work, including fractures, sprains, and strains."[6] If workers are injured during a delivery, their status as a private contractor and their reliance on tips often forces them to lean on friends and family members when they cannot ride—and as independent contractors, few have access to health insurance. Many delivery workers also "depend on the goodwill of bicycle mechanic friends or sympathetic bike shops to keep them working (and thus eating) as their bicycles wear out from near constant use."[7]

The instituting of surge pricing to incentivize delivery workers to go online during "peak" periods had only made it more dangerous for the workers.[8] Peak periods are often during moments of inclement weather, rainy days, and blizzards. In extreme instances, the consequences of racing for tips, especially during inclement weather, can be fatal. Caviar couriers have shared that during torrential downpours they have received an encouraging "peppy, emoji-adorned message" from the company that reads "when it rains the orders POUR on Caviar! . . . Go online ASAP to cash in!"[9] On a rainy afternoon in 2018, during a moment of surge pricing, a young Caviar delivery worker was racing to drop off orders when he was struck and killed by a car.[10] Caviar, like other delivery platforms, profits "off the vulnerability of independent contractors much the way . . . restaurants have long profited off the vulnerability of" tipped workers.[11]

Working as a delivery worker has long meant facing dangerous working conditions. But the gig economy has amplified existing dangers and inequalities, by adopting and proliferating the subminimum wage while eliminating traditional protections. Many platform-based workers now depend on tips to make ends meet, with tips at times comprising nearly 100 percent of take-home pay.

Traditionally tipped industries have created a new model—one that other industries looking to skirt the traditional responsibilities of an employer have emulated. Tech corporations' use of the subminimum wage is only the tip of the iceberg. The emerging industry's embrace of a subminimum wage signals the growing use of tips as wage replacement across many different sectors. As long as the subminimum wage for tipped workers is allowed to persist, the country runs the risk of seeing new categories of workers enter the subminimum wage universe.

8

Angel

Driving for the Subminimum

"They give you very little as a company"

Angel had a severe mental breakdown in the summer of 2019.

He was walking through the woods with his partner, he remembers. "It was cold. For some reason, it was chilly, like it was like the beginning of spring. And I remember taking my jacket off, taking all of my jewelry off, and grabbing the biggest log that I could pick up, and just slamming it on the ground continuously, yelling at the top of my lungs, not giving a f★ck if I was damaging my voice." You could hear Angel's voice echoing. He'd never experienced anything like that outpouring of emotion. "I was just so angry and so frustrated with everything, just yelling." His partner "took a step back and allowed me to do my thing. And when I was done, I just cried. I [was] down on my knees just crying, calling my father . . . not knowing what to do with my life and not knowing where to go."

Angel is a singer and teacher who grew up in Lancaster, a city of sixty thousand about seventy miles from Philadelphia,

Pennsylvania. His family hails from Piedras Negras and San Germán, Puerto Rico—a territory of the United States. "It's an interesting thing, being a Puerto Rican here, because even other Latinos will tell you that you're American, but our experiences are the same . . . getting treated different-ly. You know, my dad was getting held back and flunked. He was a really smart guy, but they thought he was stupid because he spoke Spanish."

Angel comes from a family of musicians. His dad and three of his older uncles were in a trio playing música jíbara, the folk music of Puerto Rico, up and down the East Coast. Eventually much of the family settled in Lancaster as part of the Puerto Rican diaspora, drawn by agricultural and manufacturing jobs. Uncles on his mom's side worked at High Steel installing bridges and other industrial projects.

Puerto Rico, along with Guam and the Philippines, became an American territory when it was ceded by Spain at the conclusion of the Spanish-American War in 1898. Puerto Ricans were granted citizenship through an Act of Congress twenty years later, in 1917, and the island is now a Commonwealth that can elect its own governor but cannot vote for president or congressional representatives.

Angel left when he was nineteen to attend the University of the Arts in Philadelphia, "And I just never looked back."

University of the Arts was his dream school, and even though he got a scholarship, he had to take out student loans to get by. He didn't really understand loan interest at the time. In his mind, "I'm going to the college of my dreams. I need to make that happen no matter what."

His parents encouraged him to go to college, but they wanted him to go to a smaller school near Lancaster. "I had a scholarship to go to Millersville University. . . . A lot of people that go to my high school graduate and go to that college. I'm just glad, you know, regardless of the debt that I have, I'm glad I didn't go, you know."

The dorms were "stupidly expensive," so he lived with roommates in North, West, and South Philly, moving every year.

"South Philly," Angel explains, "has been a historically Black [neighborhood] for a long time. It was wonderful. Even though the crime was pretty high, and sometimes it could be a little scary, the sense of community was very large." North Philadelphia was the same way. "They were very . . . slow to [accept you, asking], 'Who's this guy?' But once they see what you're about, then they accept you with open arms. And it's one of the most welcoming communities that I've ever had the pleasure to be a part of."

After graduation, he was easily able to get work teaching music in charter schools geared toward Latino students and taught for ASPIRA and Esperanza academies, as well as Latin Jazz at Amla, a nonprofit Latin music school. Most of Angel's students were Latino, primarily Puerto Rican, Dominican, Colombian, and Mexican.

Angel loved teaching in North Philly. "It can be a little

bit taxing, and it can take a lot of energy. . . . Because there's a lot of trauma within that part of the city. But it is also very rewarding." Driving through the neighborhood, Angel could see the trauma. And in school the kids and their families would look to him as a mentor, and the students would tell him about their experiences. "When you care for somebody, and you find out that their dad is being abusive, or one of their cousins got shot and killed, or their brother's killed, or they're living in an abandoned building, or they're homeless, those things affect you."

Teaching in this difficult environment, however, was exhausting and poorly paid. And so like many working people in a broad range of professions, Angel turned to Uber to supplement his income and give him greater flexibility. Angel needed to pay his bills. He figured he could start working at Uber and take his music career more seriously.

Working at Uber was too easy. "They know that a person who's not making a lot of money and is struggling financially can come up with $250. It's difficult but not impossible. You come up with $250 and you walk away with a brand new car and the ability to make money. It is very, very attractive." Angel quickly added, "But it's also very destructive."

Prior to the invention of the taximeter, passengers would hail cabriolets, or cabs—single horse-drawn carriages for human transport. The taximeter was invented in 1891, allowing for measurement of time and distance to standardize fares, and the taxicab was born. By the end of the nine-teenth century, there were one hundred taxicabs in New York. The idea then spread across the country. Checker Cab was founded in Joliet, Illinois, in 1922 and quickly became the prototypical American taxi. As with carryout food, taxis were concentrated at rail terminals, hotels, and other nexuses of commerce, travel, and human migration flows.

For decades, taxi drivers have been classified as independent contractors under a system where they would lease cabs from a cab company for a set fee and keep fares and tips. Most cities have historically limited the number of taxicabs through city permits, known as medallions, which due to their scarcity could reach values of hundreds of thousands of dollars. As a result, investment firms would purchase the medallions for lease. Some individuals also purchased medallions, in effect becoming owner-operators. Many taxi drivers fell victim to medallion purchases at exorbitant prices financed through predatory lenders. Now, with the proliferation of ride-sharing apps, many of these medallions plummeted in value, leaving these taxi drivers penniless and leading many to commit suicide out of desperation.

Medallions were a once highly coveted commodity that held the promise of a comfortable existence. Now, for many, they are a harbinger of financial ruin.

In 2009, a computer programmer named Garrett Camp came up with the idea to launch Uber after he had spent

$600 for a private ride home on New Year's Eve. He teamed up with Travis Kalanick, who became the company's first CEO, and together with other programmers Camp built the first prototype. In 2010 they hired their first employee, Ryan Graves, who was named general manager and received 5 to 10 percent shares in the business. By 2013, the company was operating in twenty-three cities; by 2014 the company was launching worldwide. The company went public in 2019, but almost immediately announced $5.6 billion in loss and the layoff of over eight hundred Uber employees.

Despite these wild fluctuations, Uber has led the explosion of the ride-sharing business. In less than a decade, ride-hailing services such as Uber and Lyft have disrupted the lives of thousands of taxi drivers, crowding the streets with thousands more drivers jockeying for fares.

The Uber system is built on "a little bit of deceit." Angel explains: "Uber says rent this car, and then you can make up to $20 an hour. Well, you got to pay $150 a week for that. And then you got to pay for gas. They're not giving you anything. Everything is coming out of your pocket." Uber encourages its drivers to provide gum and water to customers, "if you want a five-star rating and tips." Uber doesn't reimburse those expenses, so $20 an hour quickly goes down to $10 to $12 an hour or less, "depending on the day."

After around four miles, drivers can expect to earn $1 a mile, Angel relates. "I can expect if I'm going to have a ten-mile, eleven-mile ride, that's going to be about $12 to $13 that I'll get."

Since Uber drivers are independent contractors, they aren't guaranteed any earnings. There are times that Angel has been out for an hour or an hour and a half, "and I won't get a ride at all. . . . But technically, since you are an independent contractor, they don't guarantee you any work." As a result, "there's some days where I made $7 an hour."

There is also a learning curve for drivers about precautions they must take as independent contractors. "You know, they're not taking your taxes out. A lot of people aren't educated on that. I wasn't educated on that. I know it sounds stupid. . . . I should have a better knowledge of finances, but I don't know, I'm just a musician. It's taken me a while to really understand that part." As an independent contractor, each Uber driver must handle their own self-employment taxes, possibly with estimated quarterly payments to not run afoul of the IRS—and should factor in the cost of a tax advisor. "And Uber is not liable for any of it," Angel adds.

When Uber first began operations, it advertised a tip-free service as one of its selling points and discouraged riders from offering and drivers from accepting tips. After several lawsuits challenging that practice—since Uber drivers are independent contractors, and since Lyft, Uber's primary competitor, offered in-app tipping for years—Uber began slowly rolling out in-app tipping as mandated by law and market conditions.

Angel saw this change in real time. "When I started working at Uber, there were no tips. People paid you in cash if they wanted to tip you, which was very rare. I had a pretty high rating, 4.95 or something like that. It fluctuates, it might have gone down to 4.91, but, for the most part, I had a really high rating. I got a lot of compliments from people, but I didn't get tips often, if at all." Now, Uber makes a big deal of tipping on the app. "Oh yeah, now you get a notification saying, 'Oh, you received a tip, here's $1.' 'Ooh, you received a tip,' but I might have twenty rides, and I might still only get two or three tips."

It appears that very few people tip. Although Uber states that workers receive all of their tips, they have not made clear that drivers receive the tip in its entirety without off-setting their guaranteed compensation. As Angel explains, "Yeah, if I made $20, and somebody gave me a tip, there's no way for us to really know if they're taking anything."

Uber drivers can wait to receive payment once a week, or they can opt for a pay-now system.

"If I work today, and I made $70 today, then I can just say pay now. And I can get paid in a couple of seconds, which is pretty nice. They take 50 cents [for the company] each time you do that, but it goes into your bank account."

Angel sees the tips as a double-edged sword. Tips can confer advantages, and have the potential for an increase in weekly earnings. But on the other hand, "Uber, they don't give you a lot. They give you very little as a company . . . okay, you're getting tips now, but there's still no security."

Uber does not have a hiring structure, and Angel complains that the roads are being inundated with Uber drivers. Angel describes the hiring process: "Yo, you got a car that works? Cool." Angel finds there is a classist element to the Uber system as well, of drivers being required to use newer cars in order to maintain a certain aesthetic standard—forcing many drivers to rent cars rather than use their own. "I understand why they would want to have cars that are newer. I understand that as a business model, but the avenues for renting cars are so awful. You could have zero dollars in the account, but if you can just come up with a certain amount of money, you can drive a car today. And that's dope, on paper, but the risks are so high."

Uber drivers used to depend on surge pricing—higher fees during rush hour and other high demand time periods—to make a little extra bit of money, but now, Angel says, "there's an oversaturation of drivers in the market, so there's very little opportunities for surges." Along with the reduction in surge pricing, increasing the number of drivers also decreases the amount of money workers can make on a standard day, too. "There were times where you could drop somebody off, and while you were dropping somebody off, you'd get another [fare]. So it would just be continuous."

The conditions for drivers have also deteriorated as the number of Uber drivers has increased, creating opportunities for accidents. Angel complains, "The roads are just sh★t now because people are just trying to make money. They're double parking in weird places that are very dangerous, cutting across traffic, no turn signals. A lot of times, when I'm driving, and I see something stupid on the road, I will see an Uber sticker."

Angel has also noticed a change in the relationship between drivers and riders. "I used to have a lot of conversations. I used to do a lot of networking from Uber. And now, people just don't want to talk. It used to be this experience, you know, 'Oh, wow, I'm in this Uber.' I used to curate my music and play very specific types of music that I knew most people don't hear or don't know of. Now they put on their headphones, they don't acknowledge you. 'Take me to my place.' And that's it." Angel has had days without a single conversation.

The misclassification of Uber drivers as independent contractors led Angel into a Kafkaesque nightmare. When he started driving, Uber offered him a three-year lease on a brand-new car for $250 down. He had to pay $154 per week, and he could return the car with two weeks' notice.

The arrangement worked well until Angel had to stop driving because he got sick—and unlike all other workers in Philadelphia, as an independent contractor he did not have access to the city mandated benefit of paid sick days. Every day not working meant a day of lost pay. After two weeks with the flu, Angel says, "I started falling behind on payments, and that's where it gets very scary. You start falling behind on payments, then you're talking about $150 a week, then you gotta pay $300, then you gotta pay $700. And then, before you know it . . .

Angel's car was repossessed—which led him further down a financial hole. "When I got my car repoed, I came up with the money to get the car back. And they charge you like a stupid fee. I owed maybe $500." Angel went to pay the fee but was told he needed to send a certified check by overnight mail. He borrowed the money to get the car back and he was told he would get the car back within twenty-four to forty-eight hours.

"So then the weekend came, they still didn't get my car. Saturday came, they still didn't get my check. So this is the whole week that I wasn't working, and just stacking up money." When they finally acknowledged his check, they gave him the address of the place to pick it up. They wouldn't release the car until he paid $700 in towing fees. Angel was exasperated. "I was working, trying to catch up, and trying to catch up on my regular bills, and I just couldn't do it. There was no way that I could catch up with the lease that I owed, and then still keep the rent, and then still keep my electric on, and then I got it repoed again." He gave up on Uber because of the stress.

He gets calls from a collection agency for the money he

still owes on the car, but he isn't sure how to deal with it. "If they're trying to get me to pay for the rest of the lease, which could be like $15,000, I don't have that. There's no way that I can pay that."

He has taken up Uber again to try to get back on his feet through a car share called Getaround that rents to Uber drivers by the hour. The cars come equipped with car mounts for the windshield emblem and auxiliary cables and chargers. "At first, it was a pretty good deal. It was $5 an hour to rent a car, which, if you're taking into account wear and tear, it's actually a little bit cheaper than using your own car." However, the fee has changed to a "flexible kind of pay structure that goes upwards, from 5 to 7 to 8 to 9 to 10 dollars." The cars are new, so they are more efficient and it costs less to fill the tank. "I drove for seven hours, and only had to pay $12 to refill the tank." On Saturday, when he can make the most money, it adds up to about $20 an hour. "And if you're talking about paying 7, 8, 9 dollars an hour for a car, and that goes down to $11 an hour. And then if you're talking about paying $12 for gas, then it's just awful. I'm doing it now out of necessity, because I have nothing else."

Angel recognizes that driving Uber is completely individualistic. "You know, there's nothing, there's no community within Uber. You are doing it for you. For you, that's it. . . . Yes, you're taking people from point A to point B. I guess that's a service, but it's never fulfilled me. It's just a thing to do to make a couple of bucks."

Angel believes that Uber, and "all of those gig jobs, every single one of them, are bordering on straight-up slavery. I think the way we are going towards a society where everything is going towards convenience . . . where people [say], well, I can order beer from my couch, I can order whatever I want from my couch, and it'll come to my front door. That is so alluring to the consumer that they're not taking into account that, okay, well my Uber is cheap as sh★t now? Well, that's because we can't make any money. On paper Uber says, well, you just made $20 an hour, but they have no liability. So, everything that the consumer is getting with convenience, none of that is going on the shoulders of the corporation itself. It's going on the shoulders of the people that are actually providing you the service. And, more and more people are competing . . . they're all undercutting themselves, just to get a piece of the market. And they're making it so that these jobs are basically minimum wage type shifts. I'm very afraid to see what the job market is going to become in the next ten years because of the gig economy."

9

Frances and Fiona

Workers with Disabilities and Youth Workers Want Equal Pay

"We have a voice"

Frances Mablin is an African American woman who was born and grew up in a mixed community in Little Rock, Arkansas. Frances was born with cerebral palsy and was raised by her grandmother until she was ten. "My grandmother did it mostly all on her own. She tried to get me in therapy—she had people coming in and out of the house, but none of it worked."

Frances's grandmother passed when she was ten years old, and Frances was moved into a group home in Little Rock. There she received more regular therapy and counseling. "I learned to do for myself, live on my own, learn independently. It was important for my future." Frances attended a public middle school at first, but her caseworker felt it would not be a good idea as she did not have an aide at school, and so Frances started attending school at the group home itself.

When Frances was old enough to go to high school, she went to live with her grandmother's sister in Osceola,

Arkansas. She was in a special education class in the high school, where she reunited with some of her friends and classmates from childhood. Frances thrived in high school and finally graduated in 2002 at the age of seventeen, just before her eighteenth birthday. "My family from the group home came, along with my classmates and friends. I was happy and proud. I was one of the first to graduate from high school in my family. It felt great. It let me know I could do anything if I wanted to, if I put my mind to it."

Just before she graduated from high school, Frances's grandmother's sister passed away, and she went to live with her father. "My dad put me out. He couldn't take care of me. The school nurse said I needed an appointment for a physical exam and to sign a permission slip to participate in sports. He didn't want to sign the slip or take me to see the doctor, so we had a disagreement and he put me out."

Frances was sent back to the group home, but post-graduation she wanted to learn a trade, and there was no place to do so in Osceola. Her social worker sent her to a vocational counselor who got her a place at the Arkansas Career Institute in Hot Springs, Arkansas. "I was so excited—it was good. I just wanted a job—anything I could do with my hands. I needed a job to support myself." Frances was enrolled in a machinery certificate program, in which she learned to assemble tanks on lawnmowers. She lived on campus. "There were people there from all walks of life. It was great—I made friends. I had a roommate. Me and my roommate became the best of friends. She was from a different part of Arkansas, and she didn't have a disability, but she was also learning machinery."

After the first year at the institute, Frances moved off

campus and got her own apartment for the first time. "It was my first time living by myself. I was nervous and excited at the same time. I really didn't know anybody in the apartment complex. I had to get to know people. I'm not really a shy person; I'm very vocal about what I need and want. But I was nervous and excited about being able to be on my own; I had to prove to myself that I could do it. So many people said I wouldn't be able to live on my own. To prove them wrong was a great thing."

Around the time Frances completed her machinery course, she got back in touch with her mother. She moved to Blytheville, Arkansas, to be with her. "My mom didn't raise me, and I wanted to rekindle things with her." She stayed with her mother for about six months, and then moved back to Little Rock to get a job.

Back home in Little Rock, Frances got her first job at Goodwill. Frances's vocational counselor enrolled her in a one-year contract with Goodwill, with the promise to move her into a different occupation at the end of the year. "It was my first paid job. I was excited about that." When she first started, Frances was paid the full minimum wage in Arkansas of $7.25. But after the first paycheck, Goodwill changed her pay structure. "Starting in the second pay period we were paid by production. If we processed three big totes of donations an hour, we could make around $60 a week." Frances was working forty hours per week, which meant she was being paid $1.50 an hour—a subminimum wage because she was a person with a disability. "I think they start you off on the full minimum wage to get you in the program, and then they change the pay."

Frances was living in her own apartment in Little Rock, but her income from her full-time job at Goodwill did not provide enough to cover her rent. She was still reliant on public assistance at a time when she hoped to finally become self-sufficient.

Frances said the pay "didn't work very well. It made me feel disturbed. It was my first job, so I tried to hang in there. I was angry, but I didn't let my anger show. Some people might have been okay with the pay because they had their parents or someone to fall back on. With me, I had to fend for myself. There were other people like me who had to fend for themselves. They didn't like it either, but they didn't complain, because they were worried about losing their jobs."

Goodwill is a nonprofit organization that processes castaway clothing and goods and recycles them to sell in a second-hand store, which produces revenue for the organization. Goodwill has been criticized for its problematic business model of "sheltered workshops," workplaces in which people with disabilities are legally segregated from other workers and paid subminimum wages based solely on their disability. "The supervisors and coworkers were respectful, but the building was old, stuffy, with no air and no windows. We were in a big warehouse room. There were concrete floors, totes on wheels, and people standing around a conveyer belt, getting the stuff, putting it into totes, and pushing it to you."

At the end of the year at Goodwill, Frances's vocational counselor did not produce the promised next job. Frances attempted to apply to stay at Goodwill, but they rejected her.

Around this time, Frances was asked by her family to move to Memphis, Tennessee, to help care for her father, who was now ailing and suffered from seizures. "My siblings in Tennessee weren't helping with my dad. They wanted to do their own thing. I was left to care for him before he died." Frances moved in with her father and a family friend, who became the primary caregiver; she needed Frances's help to care for her father until he passed away. Since then, Frances has stayed in Memphis, applying for various jobs, but being rejected from every one so far. "In Memphis, they're not hiring people with my kind of disability. I tried to go to Goodwill, but they wouldn't hire me, not to work in their stores." Frances's dream would be to do any kind of work with children, which she also applied for, but she got turned down for that as well.

Opponents of One Fair Wage for people with disabilities argue that since few people will hire those with disabilities, as Frances has found, employers like Goodwill must be allowed to pay a subminimum wage as an incentive to provide any jobs to people like Frances who have disabilities. But Frances does not agree that that justifies a subminimum wage for people with disabilities. "I think it's horrible. People with disabilities should be treated as equal to other people. We should get the minimum wage. Some of us have to pay for transportation. We have to buy clothes, buy food, things we need or things we like, like everyone else."

So why is there a subminimum wage for people with disabilities? Frances thinks it is a matter of power. "The only reason they get away with it is because no one has spoken up. They know we're desperate for work, that other people won't hire us."

For Frances, having a job that would pay her a full minimum wage is a matter of survival. "If I were paid minimum wage, I would get new eyeglasses. I need new eyeglasses. Medicaid will cover either an eye exam or new eyeglasses. Being able to see to cross the road—that would make a big difference. Right now, to get on the bus, read the signs—it's hard for me now. I take someone with me if I decide to go somewhere."

But having a job that would pay her a full minimum wage would also allow her to enjoy some very basic aspects of a full human life that most other Americans enjoy. "If I earned a full minimum wage, I would save to go on a trip. I have family I haven't seen in years, in Florida, Atlanta, Chicago. I'd like to go see my family."

Most importantly, though, Frances, like most other people, would love to have children. "I'm thirty-six now; I'll be thirty-seven in June. I would love to find a job so I could get extended health insurance to see if I could have children. You have to get a lot of referrals through Medicaid, so by the time you get through all that, you're like, 'Forget it.'"

But Frances persists; she says she will keep trying to find a job, and keep trying to see if she can have children. "I haven't given up. Children have always been my passion. I have more patience with children than I do adults. I know that may sound crazy. I want my legacy to live on, even after I'm gone."

Fiona Joseph was born in Livingston, New Jersey, and raised nearby. Her grandmother had immigrated from rural Haiti to New Jersey in the 1970s on her own, looking for work and a better life for her family. Over time she was able to bring her sons—Fiona's father and uncles. Fiona's father came to the United States at the age of thirteen and went to high school and a New Jersey state college, after which he worked a wide range of jobs—financial advisor, security guard, operations manager. When it came time to get married, Fiona's father decided to move back to Haiti, where he met and fell in love with Fiona's mother, and ultimately sponsored her to come back to New Jersey. By this time, Fiona's uncles had started their own families. So by the time Fiona was born, her family had grown over several neighboring counties in the state.

"I was an only child, but I had lots of cousins—dozens of cousins—old, young, everyone. The big thing about my

family is that they are really close. So even though it might sound weird to people, I was really close to my second and third cousins." Being located in New Jersey counties close to New York, beyond her cousins, Fiona enjoyed growing up in a sizable Haitian community.

Fiona's parents sacrificed a great deal to make sure she could get a good education. Her mother drove her thirty minutes every day to school, after which she herself had to drive another hour to her job as a nurse. "A majority of my friends at school in Elizabeth, New Jersey, were Latinx, Spanish speakers, but the school also had a mix of Black, white, and Asian people." Fiona enjoyed school. "I've always been a positive person, viewing people from a positive note. It's the Haitian mentality—you work hard."

Fiona's positivity also resulted in her taking on leadership roles in school. "I was junior class president and student body class president. I was volunteering in lots of different organizations, and ended up at Make the Road New Jersey in my junior year." Make the Road New Jersey is a nonprofit organization that builds the power of immigrant and working-class communities to achieve dignity and respect. Fiona's friends in high school told her about Make the Road's college access program at their Student Success Center, in which students were invited to a ten-week intensive program to learn about college and financial aid.

"I was in English class, my last period of the day, and class ended early so some of the kids were talking to each other. One of my friends, Rudy, told me to go to the Student Success Center because it was college application season. I said, 'I'm a junior, calm down.' But he showed me a flyer and encouraged me to go, and I was interested so I decided to apply to go."

Fiona's parents were not able to help her figure out the college application process, so she was interested in learning more but also nervous. "When I first went there it was very nerve-racking. It was a very different place than I was used to. I remember walking to their office—it was a long staircase down to where the meeting was going to be held, and it felt more and more nerve-racking with every step down.

But later on I found that this is where I found my friends, found my community."

While going through the Student Success Center's ten-week boot camp, Fiona learned about other meetings held at the center that were run by youth. "I started attending other meetings and realizing they were not so scary. There were youth actually organizing, working on different campaigns. I remember learning about their driver's license campaign. They'd ask me 'Are you interested in going to a march? Canvassing opportunities?' I was able to integrate myself more into the organizing work."

In spring 2018 Fiona learned about the Fight for $15, a broad coalition effort to raise the minimum wage in New Jersey to $15 an hour. Although New Jersey had one of the lowest state minimum wages in the region, New Jersey's newly elected governor, Phil Murphy, had campaigned through 2018 on the promise of a $15 minimum wage. Fiona was outraged to hear that not everyone would benefit from the raise if enacted. "When we were talking about it as a big group, I learned that there would be subminimum wages for some people, and that the way that they were planning on it, tens of thousands of people in New Jersey would be left out of the $15 minimum wage. As soon as they started talked about subtiers for tipped workers, and youth, and farmworkers, I was like, 'No!' You think policymakers do things based on common sense, but the subtiered system was just whack."

The notion of a subminimum wage for teens particularly hit home for Fiona, who was sixteen years old and had just started her first job. "In fall 2017 I knew I needed a job. . . . I had personal bills I had to pay for, and I felt bad that knowing my parents are not a money tree. They were struggling, too, and I knew that I couldn't leech off them. They had their own responsibilities and unexpected costs. . . . One of our cars broke down, and my parents were spending thousands of dollars trying to revive their car. The car was just not working. Thousands of dollars were lost—for naught. And meanwhile I had my phone bills, and I was taking AP [Advanced Placement] classes, so I had to buy flashcards, study guides, books they offer at $25 a pop. Buying books was expensive to study for the SAT, and I was trying to do well. It would amount to hundreds of dollars."

Unlike more affluent families, Fiona's parents were not in a position to help finance her educational costs—they were barely able to cover their own. "Sometimes my parents would need a loan of $100 to make ends meet. Unexpected things happened—the best example was our family car. . . . My mother works an hour away from where we live, and the car breaking down made the commute impossible. I wanted to save up for college—I didn't know how financial aid works, it was really complex. Even applying to college was expensive—each application cost $70 to $90, and I wanted to apply to lots of schools. It was adding up to like $1,000, just not feasible for my parents."

Fiona started by applying to jobs at the mall, where most of her friends worked. She filled out lots of applications and started sending them out, but never heard back. "It was really frustrating. I was sixteen, and the retailer preferred older kids." Finally, in April 2018, a local movie theater offered Fiona an entry-level crew member position, in which she would serve as an usher, clean the theater, greet guests, scan tickets, sell concessions, and prepare popcorn. The job was fifteen hours per week, $8.60 per hour. "Initially, I was like 'Wow, yay, I have a job!' But then I was a little disappointed that the minimum wage was so low, even though I was grateful to get a job. But . . . I needed the money."

Fiona had been attending meetings of the Youth Power Project at Make the Road New Jersey every Monday, where she learned that legislators were proposing to create a subminimum wage for youth within the new $15 minimum wage bill. "I was completely outraged about the subminimum wage—it was confusing and unfair. They were excluding tipped workers, and I knew from the experience of my other friends that tipped wages were not enough to make ends meet. As a youth worker, I was angry. Given the context of my job, where you had young people working in the movie theater ranging from sixteen to thirty, I thought of it the same way—if I was stationed at a concession stand next to someone who was twenty-one, I'd be making less than them when I'd be doing just the same work—making the popcorn, talking to guests, ringing up orders. If we're doing the exact same work, how is it fair at all that they're being [paid] $15 an hour, and I'm being paid $8. Youth work wasn't being valued. Work is work regardless."

At first, New Jersey legislature proposed cutting teenage workers—aged fourteen to eighteen—completely out of the $15 minimum wage bill. In the second version of the bill, they proposed that teen workers would eventually get to $15 an hour, but not until 2036. Other workers would get to $15 an hour by 2026. "With inflation, by 2036, that would be the equivalent of what I'm making today." Fiona was particularly outraged because many of her peers were using their income to support their families. "One of my peers gave their entire check from work to their parents to pay the rent. Their mother was a tipped worker and couldn't afford the rent. One of my other friend's checks was going to pay the rent and save up for a car. They were walking miles to go to work and they were saving up so they could drive." Many of Fiona's friends lived in New Jersey residential neighborhoods very far from any mass transit access. "Another one of my friends used her wages to pay for school uniforms for her younger sister and herself, because they were expensive. And she gave portions of her money to her mother to pay rent, bills, utilities." In multiple cases, Fiona's teenage friends' wages from work were needed to cover family bills, including rent and groceries for the family to be able to eat.

Despite the fact that so many of Fiona's teenage peers were counting on their income for survival, New Jersey legislators argued that they should receive a subminimum teen wage as an "apprenticeship" or training experience. They argued that for teenagers, it was more important to be able to learn soft skills and a sense of responsibility, rather than be paid a standard wage. "The idea of youth working as a training experience or learning experience rather than someone actually trying to pay their bills—for me, it made no sense. The people I knew who were teens were working to pay bills to supplement their parents' income. Instead of trying to support these youth, these legislators were excluding tons of youth who needed the actual minimum wage. It completely didn't make sense. Their arguments seemed to be based on data that was made up as opposed to the stories of people I knew, myself included."

The National Employment Law Project (NELP) issued a report that confirmed Fiona's experience, indicating that 40 percent of teens who work as low-income workers contributed at least 20 percent of their household income. The report also indicated that more than 80 percent of these low-income teens are young women of color.

Fiona and the Youth Power Project moved into action. "We did a lot. One of the first things we did was circulate a petition. Ten or twenty of us would go to different locations across New Jersey, from Perth Amboy to Asbury Park, asking people to sign a petition for youth not to be carved out of the minimum wage. We amassed six thousand signatures.

We also did a lot of powerful social media—including live streaming videos of a group of us dispelling the myths of the teen minimum wage."

The group wrote op-eds in local papers and created a video on Halloween to talk about how "scary" it was to carve youth out of the minimum wage. They also organized light projections onto malls across the state. "Since a large majority of youth workers work at the mall, we were able to put out projections with the faces of kids in Make the Road New Jersey and their wages, and why they wanted a real minimum wage."

The group also visited legislators. "We delivered six thousand signatures to Senate President Sweeney in lots of boxes of signed petitions." At first, state police intervened and wouldn't let Fiona and her peers deliver the petitions. But because the youth had amassed a large social media following of schoolkids and their allies, when they blasted on Twitter that the Senate president would not receive their petitions, Senate President Sweeney responded within fifteen minutes saying he'd come and receive the petitions. "He actually met with us, but he said he couldn't support us."

Fiona and her peers did not give up. "We delivered petitions to every legislator, with teens being followed around by cameras." And they kept up the projections on malls, especially during the holidays, highlighting how teens were being overworked and abused because of the holiday shopping crowd. At one point, they projected Fiona's face and story on her local mall. "The movie theater was actually next to the mall. I had to be at work in twenty minutes, but I asked them to please let me stay and watch what was going on. It was a visually stunning way to show people who were shopping, minding their own business, before they walked into the mall, they see that face—the person who's folding the clothes, giving you pretzels. It was very powerful."

They also held direct actions. "When the bill was introduced that carved us out, we held an emergency rally. From the rally we started walking around to the local stores, protesting about this issue. It got a lot of local attention. It was embarrassing for the [business owners] to say no to students and youth who wanted to be included. It gave them a lot of pressure."

Governor Murphy responded to the youth pressure. He went to visit one of Fiona's peers at his house and recorded a video in which he listened to the boy about his home life, why he needed the minimum wage, and how he was helping his mother pay for rent and bills at home.

Eventually, New Jersey legislators felt the pressure coming from all sides—from social media, direct actions, petitions, and more. By December 2018, Governor Murphy was moving for the $15 bill to be signed very quickly.

The New Jersey legislature voted to pass the $15 minimum wage bill, with no exceptions for youth, within two weeks. And the governor actually came to the Make the Road New Jersey office to sign the bill. "It was symbolic—

the same place that we worked and planned, the signing happened," Fiona said. "It reconfirmed the idea that organizing works. Organizing is real, it happens. It was a testament to young people coming together. When people come together for a common cause, they can win. At first people say it's too radical, too crazy—like the minimum wage to begin with, at first they said it was crazy. Now a $15 minimum wage is no longer crazy. It made us feel that if there's something you really want, it's achievable. Organizing was the way I saw that. It was the real-world application of putting your mind to something, and knowing we have a voice, we're being heard. You don't have to stay unheard, you can advocate for what you believe in."

Conclusion

On June 27, 1963, a twenty-four-year-old white man named William Devereux Zantzinger, a member of a wealthy tobacco farming family, ordered a drink at a hotel bar in Baltimore. Zantzinger had, by his own account, "been smacking—tapping—waitresses on the tail and they didn't say a thing. I was just playing." Others report he was using racial epithets and physically assaulting staff. When Hattie Carroll—a fifty-one-year-old Black grandmother who worked as a server—reportedly didn't bring Zantzinger's drink fast enough, Zantzinger beat her with a cane. Hattie Carroll died eight hours later. Zantzinger was eventually sentenced to six months in prison, though he was allowed to put off his sentence for two months to supervise the family crop haul.

In 1963, the wage for tipped workers like Hattie was $0 an hour, making her completely reliant on Zantzinger's tips and therefore giving him enormous power over her. Today, nearly sixty years later, the federal minimum wage for tipped workers is just $2.13 an hour—a $2 increase— and a mostly woman, disproportionately woman of color workforce of tipped workers still faces the highest levels of harassment of any industry because they must tolerate inappropriate customer behavior to earn nearly all of their income in tips—a situation that has become life-threatening during the pandemic as women are asked to remove their masks so male customers can judge their looks and their tips on that basis. But there is now so much momentum for the subminimum wage for tipped workers, which caused so much suffering for Hattie and so many other tens of millions of women like her over the last 150 years, to finally come to an end.

Subminimum wages are subhuman. They are a reflection of the value America has placed on the humanity of the people in subminimum wage sectors: tipped workers are in large majority women and especially women of color like Hattie; for workers with disabilities and youth, their subminimum wage is a direct reflection of their identity; incarcerated workers, whose subminimum wage is a direct legacy of slavery who are disproportionately brown and Black; and gig workers, who are disproportionately immigrants, women, and people of color. Only through the combined effort of all these communities will we be able to win an end to all subminimum wages in the United States.

There is now momentum to end all subminimum wages. Tipped workers, workers with disabilities, youth workers, gig workers, and incarcerated workers have been organizing for decades, and their voices are finally being heard; the Raise the Wage Act would end subminimum wages for tipped workers, workers with disabilities, and youth. Now we need to keep fighting to end all subminimum wages in the United States.

We launched the One Fair Wage campaign in 2013, after doing years of research that showed that the seven states that require One Fair Wage—California, Oregon, Washington, Nevada, Minnesota, Montana, and Alaska—have higher restaurant sales, the same or higher job growth in the restaurant industry, the same or higher tipping averages, and half the rate of sexual harassment. In 2015, restaurant industry leader Danny Meyer announced his support for One Fair Wage, moving his own restaurants beyond One Fair Wage to a gratuity-free model. Several hundred restaurants followed his lead, seeking out our help, joining forces with us, and, in some cases, moving to One Fair Wage themselves. In early 2016, we revealed research demonstrating that the subminimum wage for tipped workers was a direct legacy of slavery and a source of ongoing racial inequity for tipped workers of color. Armed with this data on the seven states and this revelation of history, we were able to start winning state victories. From 2016 to 2018, by tipped workers raising their voices in demonstrations, hearings, and in the press, and then by getting hundreds of thousands of consumers to sign petitions in support of tipped workers, we won One Fair Wage on the ballot in Maine and Washington, DC, and in the legislature in Michigan. However, with each of these three victories, the local legislature overrode the will of the people as a result of heavy lobbying from the National Restaurant Association.

In 2018, One Fair Wage received an enormous boost from #MeToo and Time's Up. After a decade of workers sharing their stories of sexual harassment in the restaurant industry, and participatory research with these workers that established that the subminimum wage for tipped workers is a major contributor to sexual harassment in the restaurant industry, our findings were featured in hundreds of media outlets, including an in-depth investigative piece in the *Washington Post*, a multimedia spread in the *New York Times*, and in-depth coverage on *20/20*, *60 Minutes*, and *Real Time with Bill Maher*.

The coverage is what initially pushed New York's Governor Cuomo to announce that he would consider making New York the eighth state to enact One Fair Wage, and then to conduct a series of intense hearings in which thousands of workers testified in support of One Fair Wage. The National Restaurant Association, for its part, hired the Trump-Pence communications firm Mercury Public Affairs to conduct a massive misinformation campaign trying to convince tipped workers that their tips would go away if their wages went up. While they were not able to convince the majority of workers of this idea—that tips are actually the same as or higher than they are in One Fair Wage states—they did manage to get restaurants to close and bring their entire staff to testify against a wage increase based on this lie. As the hearings proceeded across the state of New York, and workers brought by their employers heard our testimony, they began to understand that they had been misinformed and stopped testifying against their own wage increases. Even throughout this period, polling showed that the majority of workers and consumers always supported One Fair Wage; these workers were a vocal minority encouraged by their bosses to speak out against their own self-interest.

In 2019, thanks to the momentum produced by #MeToo and Time's Up, One Fair Wage was introduced in sixteen states and in two bills in Congress. Up until that point, we had struggled to convince many of our allies that tipped workers needed a full minimum wage with tips on top. However, after years of exposing both the racialized history of the subminimum wage and the rampant sexual harassment in the industry being due to the subminimum wage, we were able to work with a strong coalition of labor, economic, race, and gender justice allies to win One Fair Wage in the U.S. House of Representatives. We organized thousands of tipped workers nationwide to help ensure the whole passage of the Raise the Wage Act, which included a $15 minimum wage and full elimination of the subminimum wages for tipped workers, youth, and workers with disabilities—without an ultimate carveout of tipped workers, which had occurred so many times before in multiple states and Congress throughout U.S. history. The bill passed in the U.S. House of Representatives in July 2019. Although it did not move in the Senate that year, it did represent the first time since Emancipation that either house of Congress moved to eliminate the subminimum wage for tipped workers.

When tipped workers, who had been excluded for so long in so many states and at the federal level, finally got included in the $15 federal minimum wage bill, it caused us to pause and reflect. Earlier in 2019 we had released a report documenting how tech platform delivery companies such as DoorDash and Instacart are attempting to use the subminimum wage for delivery workers, who receive tips. Our research indicated that use of the subminimum wage was expanding to new sectors, particularly given the removal of regulations for tipped workers by President Trump in December 2018. We realized that we could not have integrity if we had fought for so long for tipped workers to not be excluded from the minimum wage, but then looked the other way when other sectors, like incarcerated workers and gig workers, were still excluded. We realized that we needed to build out One Fair Wage as a broader national coalition that included not only restaurant workers, but also nail salon workers, parking and airport attendants, incarcerated workers, tech platform workers, and many more. We convened a conference of all of these different workers in early 2020 and launched a vision to win.

As it did for almost every issue worldwide, 2020 changed everything. When millions of workers were laid off in restaurants across America on Friday, March 13, 2020, we jumped into action. We launched the One Fair Wage Emergency Fund on Monday, March 16, to provide cash relief to thousands of low-wage service workers; the fund has exceeded 240,000 worker applicants. We built an army of almost one thousand volunteers who are calling each worker to screen them for need, organize them to join the fight for One Fair Wage, and register them to vote. Our organizers then followed up with potential leaders to organize them into our relational voter program and, ultimately, win One Fair Wage.

Our relief fund drew in hundreds of thousands of low-wage workers, people of color, single mothers, immigrants, and young people. These workers were anxious to speak with us, not only because they were desperate for funds, but also because they were distraught and frustrated by working for years in the service industry only to find themselves completely destitute the day after their restaurants closed. In March, thousands of these workers told us that they needed the relief fund to cover the cost of groceries for their children. In July and August, these workers told us that they were going to have to steal food for their children. By fall 2020, many were facing both food and home insecurity. Many told us they did not have money for gas to get to the food bank, and that even if they did, the food available was limited and/or spoiled. One mother told us she had fed her son bread and maple syrup for weeks because that was all that was available at the food bank. Hundreds sent us photos of their electricity bills to show that they might no longer be able to be in touch with us as they might not have internet soon. Almost all workers we talked to were frustrated with the situation—most signed up to join our organization, speak to press, and register to vote.

We raised over $23 million in a few months to hand out relief to thousands of workers; we also provided individual counseling to workers regarding their unemployment benefits and finances. When thousands of workers showed up to our national and state tele-town halls and virtual rallies with congressmembers, governors, and other state legislators and made comments on our social media pages saying that they did not want to go back to work without One Fair Wage, it was a revelation. It was the first time in my twenty years of organizing that I heard so many restaurant workers refusing to go back to work without higher pay—essentially, they were striking. We moved quickly to organize live strikes around the country and created a twenty-four-foot art piece in New York, Chicago, Washington, DC, Boston, and Philadelphia called "Elena the Essential Worker," promoting her as the new Rosie the Riveter. She towered among the buildings in Times Square and Boston Commons, and we even took her on tour with workers across the State of New York to uplift the COVID-19 crisis that the subminimum wage had become.

In a new and challenging moment for organizers, the

OFW Emergency Relief Fund provided us with a clear pathway for a different kind of organizing and voter mobilization that allowed us to not only engage hard-to-reach populations civically but also develop their leadership to change the issues that needed to be changed long before the pandemic.

Fortunately, the crisis faced by workers did not go unrecognized by thousands of independent restaurant owners. The moment showed us that we could simultaneously support workers and ensure that responsible restaurant owners who cared about their workers survived the crisis—and helped to reshape the service sector going forward. In fact, several restaurant owners who previously opposed or were hesitant about One Fair Wage were now willing to work with us to commit to One Fair Wage and increased equity. For some, their eyes were opened to the unsustainability of the system; for others, the moment allowed them to break free from an old business model that they could not see how to change. Some even worked with us to design model restaurants of the future.

Based on these conversations, we worked with various governors and mayors to launch High Road Kitchens—a program in which restaurants that commit to move to One Fair Wage and greater race and gender equity voluntarily next year receive public and private dollars to re-hire their workers and repurpose themselves as community kitchens to provide free meals to those who need them. We thus provided both relief to struggling independent restaurant owners and free meals to workers and others in need and, most importantly, reshaped the sector toward equity. We raised $5 million to provide grants to over three hundred restaurants in six states—creating a network of new restaurant owner champions for One Fair Wage as state and federal policy. Once they committed to paying One Fair Wage, they became excellent advocates for state and federal policy that would create a level playing field for all restaurants to do the same.

In late summer 2020, after Joe Biden had become the nominee for president for the Democratic Party and named Kamala Harris as his running mate, the Biden-Harris campaign named One Fair Wage on three different parts of its campaign platform—the Jobs Agenda, the Racial Justice Agenda, and the Women's Agenda. Nearly twenty years of restaurant workers organizing for change was vindicated— not only were these workers heard by the presidential and vice-presidential candidates, but the intersectional nature of the issue was understood. And when President Biden named the Raise the Wage Act as part of his $1.9 trillion COVID-19 relief package that he insisted move as the very first piece of legislation Congress consider in 2021 even before his inauguration, it was further vindication that these workers' voices had been heard—that their struggles during the pandemic, from COVID exposure to #MaskualHarassment were understood as urgent COVID issues that had to be addressed simultaneous to any other forms of pandemic relief. And although we have to keep fighting to ensure all subminimum wage workers, including incarcerated workers and gig workers, receive a full minimum wage, we have come so far toward ending a legacy of slavery and source of suffering for so many millions of women and men over so many generations.

With a broader coalition, we are now working to pass One Fair Wage for all workers in many more states and, eventually, at the federal level. That can happen if consumers across America decide that they have had enough of subsidizing more than a million employers across America by paying their workers' wages through their tips and subsidizing other subminimum wage workers' existence through public assistance. They can stand with the hundreds of thousands of subminimum wage workers and supportive employers who are demanding One Fair Wage for everyone who works in America. There are three ways consumers can do this.

1. **Contact your legislator** to demand One Fair Wage for all workers—tipped workers, workers with disabilities, youth, incarcerated workers, and gig workers. You can go to OneFairWage.org, input your zip code, and send a note to your legislator.
2. **Support restaurant owners who have been championing One Fair Wage and increased equity in restaurants**, by going to www.highroadrestaurants .org.

3. Encourage your favorite restaurant owner to join the fight for equity. You can refer restaurants to join our association at www.highroadrestaurants .org.

Subminimum wages in the United States represent at least two legacies of slavery—the exception in the Thirteenth Amendment allowing for slavery in the case of incarceration, and the exclusion of millions of Black workers from the New Deal. During the last Great Depression, the New Deal attempted to stimulate the economy by providing relief to millions, including establishing, for the first time, a federal minimum wage. However, in doing so New Deal legislation codified structural racism, excluding tipped and other Black worker sectors from earning a minimum wage themselves. Now, eighty-one years later, as we face an extended economic depression of similar magnitude, Congress—and, by extension, America—has the opportunity to right our wrong and create a New Deal for Equity that would simultaneously stimulate the economy, protect the public health, and recognize the full humanity of everyone who works in America.

Acknowledgments

Thank you to Mamdouh and the One Fair Wage staff, Board, coalition partners, and allies, and most of all, the thousands of courageous worker and employer leaders for your dedication and tireless efforts to end subminimum pay in America.

Neverending thanks to my parents, sisters, and extended family, the endless support given by my life partner Zach, and my two amazing daughters, Akeela and Lina. May we end subminimum pay before they are old enough to be paid it for work.

Notes

Introduction

1. One Fair Wage, "A Persistent Legacy of Slavery: Ending the Subminimum Wage for Tipped Workers in New York as a Racial Equity Measure," July 2020, https://onefairwage.site//wp-content/uploads/2020/11/LegacyOfSlavery_5.pdf.

2. One Fair Wage, "Locked Out by Low Wages," May 2020, https://onefairwage.site//wp-content/uploads/2020/11/OFW_LockedOut_UI_COVID-19_-FINALUPDATE.pdf.

3. Michael Lynn et al., "Consumer Racial Discrimination in Tipping: A Replication and Extension," *Journal of Applied Social Psychology* 38, no. 10 (2008): 1045–60, https://ecommons.cornell.edu/bitstream/handle/1813/71558/Lynn18_Consumer_Racial_Discrimination_in_Tipping.pdf?sequence=1&isAllowed=y.

4. One Fair Wage, "Take Off Your Mask So I Know How Much to Tip You," December 2020, https://onefairwage.site/wp-content/uploads/2020/12/OFW_COVID_WorkerExp-1.pdf.

5. One Fair Wage, "Locked Out by Low Wages."

6. Restaurant Opportunities Centers United et al., "Tipped Over the Edge: Gender Inequity in the Restaurant Industry," February 13, 2012, http://rocunited.org/wp-content/uploads/2012/02/ROC_GenderInequity_F1-1.pdf. While only 7 percent of American women work in the restaurant industry, more than a third (37 percent) of all sexual harassment claims to the Equal Employment Opportunity Commission come from the restaurant industry. https://chapters.rocunited.org/wp-content/uploads/2012/02/ROC_GenderInequity_F1-1.pdf.

7. U.S. Bureau of Labor Statistics, "Quarterly Census of Employment and Wages 2015," www.bls.gov/cew, accessed August 9, 2016; U.S. Bureau of Labor Statistics, "2012 Economic Census," www.census.gov/econ, accessed August 9, 2016.

8. U.S. Bureau of Labor Statistics, "Quarterly Census of Employment and Wages 2015" and "2012 Economic Census."

9. Restaurant Opportunities Centers United, "The Gig Is Up: The New Gig Economy and the Threat of Subminimum Wages," March 2019, https://rocunited.org/wp-content/uploads/sites/7/2020/02/TheGig IsUp.pdf.

10. Saru Jayaraman, *Forked: A New Standard for American Dining* (Oxford University Press, 2016).

11. K. A. Fisher et al., "Community and Close Contact Exposures Associated with COVID-19 Among Symptomatic Adults ≥18 Years in 11 Outpatient Health Care Facilities—United States, July 2020. *Morbidity and Mortality Weekly* 69 (2020): 1258–64, https://www.cdc.gov /mmwr/volumes/69/wr/mm6936a5.htm.

12. One Fair Wage, "Take Off Your Mask So I Know How Much to Tip You."

13. One Fair Wage, "Take Off Your Mask So I Know How Much to Tip You."

14. One Fair Wage, "Take Off Your Mask So I Know How Much to Tip You."

1. The History of Subminimum Wages

1. Philip S. Foner and Ronald L. Lewis, eds., "Part V: Black Workers in Specific Trades," *The Black Worker*, Vol. 1 (Philadelphia, PA: Temple University Press, 1978), https://temple.manifoldapp.org/projects/the -black-worker-volume-5.

2. Margaret Garb, "The Great Chicago Waiter's Strike: Producing Urban Space, Organizing Labor, Challenging Racial Divides in 1890s Chicago," *Journal of Urban History* 40 (2014): 1079–98; Dorothy S. Cobble, "The Rise of Waitressing: Feminization, Expansion, and Respectability," in *Dishing It Out: Waitresses and Their Unions in the Twentieth Century* (Champaign: University of Illinois Press, 1991).

3. Kerry Segrave, *Tipping: An American Social History of Gratuities* (Jefferson, NC: McFarland, 2011), 17.

4. Lawrence Tyre, "Choosing Servility to Staff America's Trains," *The Alicia Patterson Foundation*, May 2011, https://aliciapatterson.org /stories/choosing-servility-staff-americas-trains.

5. Restaurant Opportunities Centers United, "Our Tips Belong to

Us: Overcoming the National Restaurant Association's Attempt to Steal Workers' Tips, Perpetuate Sexual Harassment, and Maintain Racial Exploitation," October 23, 2017; National Restaurant Association, "About Us," 2021, https://restaurant.org/about.

6. Restaurant Opportunities Centers United Analysis of United States Census 1850–2010, https://rocunited.org/wp-content/uploads/sites/7/2020/07/GreatServiceDivide_Seattle_Report_W.pdf.; IPUMS-USA, University of Minnesota, https://usa.ipums.org/usa.

7. R. R. Wright Jr., "The Negro in Unskilled Labor," *Annals of the American Academy of Political and Social Science* 49, no. 1, 19–27 (first published 1913), https://www.jstor.org/stable/1011903?seq=1#metadata_info_tab_contents.

8. Daniel Levinson Wilk, "The Historical Precedent for Fast-Food Strikes," *Aljazeera America*, December 21, 2013, http://america.aljazeera.com/opinions/2013/12/fast-food-historymcdonaldswaiters.html; Margaret Garb, "The Great Chicago Waiter's Strike: Producing Urban Space, Organizing Labor, Challenging Racial Divides in 1890s Chicago," *Journal of Urban History* 40 (2014): 1079–98; Dorothy S. Cobble, "The Rise of Waitressing: Feminization, Expansion, and Respectability," in *Dishing It Out: Waitresses and Their Unions in the Twentieth Century* (Champaign: University of Illinois Press, 1991).

9. *New York Times*, "Editorial Article 1—In Maryland, by Authority of the Democratic Majority in the Legislature," April 4, 1910.

10. R. Needleman, "Tipping as a Factor in Wages," *Monthly Labor Review* 45 (December 1937): 1303–22.

11. Restaurant Opportunities Centers United Analysis of United States Census 1850–2010; IPUMS-USA, University of Minnesota, https://rocunited.org/wp-content/uploads/sites/7/2020/07/GreatServiceDivide_Seattle_Report_W.pdf.

12. Restaurant Opportunities Centers United, "The Gig Is Up."

13. One Fair Wage Analysis of the American Community Survey (2015–2019). Population currently employed in the restaurant industry with a birthplace outside of the United States and United States territories. IPUMS-USA, University of Minnesota.

14. J. M. Krogstad et al., "A Majority of Americans Say Immigrants Mostly Fill Jobs U.S. Citizens Do Not Want," *Pew Research Center*, June 10, 2020, https://www.pewresearch.org/fact-tank/2020/06/10/a

-majority-of-americans-say-immigrants-mostly-fill-jobs-u-s-citizens
-do-not-want.

15. Krogstad et al., "A Majority of Americans Say Immigrants Mostly Fill Jobs U.S. Citizens Do Not Want."

16. Bridgit Katz, "Remains of 95 African-American Forced Laborers Found in Texas," *Smithsonian Magazine*, July 19, 2018, https://www.smithsonianmag.com/smart-news/remains-95-african-american -forced-laborers-found-texas-180969703.

17. Equal Justice Initiative, "Prison Labor and the Thirteenth Amendment," February 1, 2016, https://eji.org/news/history-racial-injustice -prison-labor.

18. Grant Whittington, "Colorado Votes to Abolish Unpaid Prison Work, But Paltry Wages Are Still the Norm Nationwide," *Triple Pundit*, November 9, 2018, https://www.triplepundit.com/story/2018 /colorado-votes-abolish-unpaid-prison-work-paltry-wages-are-still -norm-nationwide/55531.

19. Wendy Sawyer, "How Much Do Incarcerated People Earn in Each State?," *Prison Policy Initiative*, April 10, 2017, https://www.prisonpolicy .org/blog/2017/04/10/wages.

20. Whittington, "Colorado Votes to Abolish Unpaid Prison Work."

21. Colleen Curry, "Whole Foods, Expensive Cheese, and the Dilemma of Cheap Prison Labor," *Vice*, July 21, 2015.

22. Ed Pilkington, "US Inmates Stage Nationwide Prison Labor Strike over 'Modern Slavery,'" *Guardian*, August 21, 2018.

23. Sawyer, "How Much Do Incarcerated People Earn in Each State?"

24. Azza Altiraifi, "Advancing Economic Security for People with Disabilities," *Center for American Progress*, July 26, 2019, https://cdn .americanprogress.org/content/uploads/2019/07/25133022/Advancing -Econ-Security-Disability-.pdf.

25. Alexia F. Campbell, "A Loophole in Federal Law Allows Companies to Pay Disabled Workers $1 an Hour," *Vox*, May 3, 2018.

26. Altiraifi, "Advancing Economic Security for People with Disabilities."

27. National Employment Law Project, "Teen Subminimum Wage: A Bad Policy That New Jersey Should Reject," June 15, 2016, https:

//www.nelp.org/publication/teen-subminimum-wage-bad-policy-that-new-jersey-should-reject.

2. Trupti

1. U.S. Bureau of Labor Statistics, "State Occupational Employment and Wage Estimates," May 2016, https://www.bls.gov/oes/current/oes_nat.htm. Analysis by the Restaurant Opportunities Centers United of wages for tipped workers in New York, Michigan, Washington, DC, OFW, and $2.13 states.

2. H. Shierholz, "Low Wages and Few Benefits Mean Many Restaurant Workers Can't Make Ends Meet," Economic Policy Institute, August 21, 2014, www.epi.org/publication/restaurant-workers.

3. Women comprise two-thirds of all restaurant workers as well as all tipped workers. Tipped restaurant workers comprise 63 percent of all tipped workers. ROC-United, National State of Tipped Workers, 2014.

4. Restaurant Opportunities Centers United.

5. Restaurant Opportunities Centers United, Forward Together, "The Glass Floor: Sexual Harassment in the Restaurant Industry," 2014.

6. Restaurant Opportunities Centers United et al., "Tipped Over the Edge."

7. Restaurant Opportunities Centers United, Sexual Harassment Focus Groups, June 2014.

8. Examining above and below average sexual harassment for all workers in the industry. Odds ratio: 7.451.

9. One Fair Wage, Professors Catharine A. MacKinnon and Louise Fitzgerald, "The Tipping Point: How the Subminimum Wage Keeps Incomes Low and Harassment High," 2021.

10. National Restaurant Association, "America Works Here," http://www.americaworkshere.org/first-job, retrieved September 19, 2014.

3. Teto

1. Langston Hughes, *The Big Sea: An Autobiography* (New York: Alfred A. Knopf, 1945).

2. U.S. Bureau of Labor Statistics, "State Occupational Employment and Wage Estimates," https://www.bls.gov/oes/current/oes_ny.htm. Customarily tipped occupations: massage therapists; bartenders; counter attendants, cafeteria, food concession, and coffee shop workers; waiters and waitresses; hosts and hostesses, restaurant, lounge, and coffee shop; food servers, non-restaurant; dining room and cafeteria attendants and bartender helpers; gaming services workers; barbers; hairdressers, hair stylists, and cosmetologists; manicurists and pedicurists; shampooers; skin care specialists; baggage porters, bellhops, and concierges; taxi drivers and chauffeurs; and parking lot attendants.

3. Jeffrey Passel, "Unauthorized Migrants: Numbers and Characteristics," Pew Research Center, June 14 2005, https://www.pewresearch.org/hispanic/2005/06/14/unauthorized-migrants.

4. Restaurant Opportunities Centers United, "The Great Service Divide: Occupational Segregation and Inequality in the US Restaurant Industry," 2014.

5. "The Great Service Divide."

6. One Fair Wage, "A Persistent Legacy of Slavery: Ending the Subminimum Wage for Tipped Workers as a Racial Equity Measure," August 2020, http://onefairwage.site/wp-content/uploads/2020/11/LegacyOfSlavery_5.pdf.

5. Yenelia

1. California Healthy Nail Salon Collaborative, "Overexposed and Underinformed: Dismantling Barriers to Health and Safety in California Nail Salons," April 2009, https://www.researchgate.net/publication/277718810_Overexposed_Under-informed_Nail_Salon_Workers_and_Hazards_to_Their_Health.

2. Statista Research Department, "Spending on Nail Salon Services in the United States from 1998 to 2017," https://www.statista.com/statistics/276605/revenuenail-salon-services-united-states.

3. New York State, "New York State's Minimum Wage Fact Sheet," https://dol.ny.gov/minimum-wage-0.

4. L. James, "Policy Report: How Safe Is Your Nail Salon?," Office of the New York City Advocate, https://www.documentcloud.org

/documents/1392469-policy-report-how-safe-is-your-nail-salon-by
-new.html.

5. U.S. Bureau of Labor Statistics, "Occupational Employment Statistics: May 2017 State Occupational Employment and Wage Estimates, Manicurists and Pedicurists—Comparison with May 2014 State Figures," https://www.bls.gov/oes/current/oes_nat.htm.

6. New York Department of Labor, "Long Term Occupational Employment Projections 2014–2024," https://www.labor.ny.gov/stats /lsproj.shtm.

7. Bureau of Labor Statistics, "Quarterly Census of Employment and Wages. Number of Workers in Establishments Primarily Engaged in Providing Nail Care Services, 2011–2016," https://data.bls.gov/cgi-bin /srgate.

8. One Fair Wage Coalition survey findings.

9. James, "Policy Report: How Safe Is Your Nail Salon?"

10. K. Barker and R. Buettner, "Nail Salon Sweeps in New York Reveal Abuses and Regulatory Challenges," *New York Times*, February 29, 2016.

11. Barker and Buettner, "Nail Salon Sweeps."

12. Bureau of Labor Statistics, "Quarterly Census of Employment and Wages."

13. Barker and Buettner, "Nail Salon Sweeps."

14. Barker and Buettner, "Nail Salon Sweeps."

15. Barker and Buettner, "Nail Salon Sweeps."

16. Barker and Buettner, "Nail Salon Sweeps."

17. Barker and Buettner, "Nail Salon Sweeps."

18. U.S. Bureau of Labor Statistics, "State Occupational Employment and Wage Estimates."

19. S. Ruggles et al., "Demographics for Foreign-Born and US-Born Tipped Workers in New York," IPUMS USA: Version 8.0, 2018, https: //doi.org/10.18128/D010.V8.0.

20. Ruggles et al., "Demographics for Foreign-Born and US-Born Tipped Workers in New York."

7. Vianne

1. U.S. Bureau of Labor Statistics, February 2019, Employment Projections, 2016–2026. See Tables 1.1 and 1.4.

2. E. Appelbaum, A. Kalleberg, and H. J. Rho, "Nonstandard Work Arrangements and Older Americans, 2005–2017," February 28, 2019, Economic Policy Institute and Center for Economic and Policy Research, https://www.epi.org/publication/nonstandard-work-arrangements-and-older-americans-2005-2017.

3. Internal Revenue Service, "Topic Number 761 Tips—Withholding and Reporting," 2019, https://www.irs.gov/taxtopics/tc761.

4. Restaurant Opportunities Centers United, "The Gig Is Up: The New Gig Economy and the Threat of Subminimum Wages," March 2019, https://rocunited.org/wp-content/uploads/sites/7/2020/02/TheGigIsUp.pdf.

5. J. Goodman, "For Deliverymen, Speed, Tips and Fear on Wheels," *New York Times*, March 2, 2012.

6. National Employment Law Project, "Gig Economy Workers Should Be Covered by Workers' Compensation," June 21, 2016, https://www.nelp.org/publication/gig-economy-workers-should-be-covered-by-workers-compensation.

7. G. Giccariello-Maher, "My Best Friend Lost His Life to the Gig Economy," *The Nation*, July 10, 2018.

8. A. Griswold, "Uber's Least Popular Feature Is Now All over Food Delivery Apps," Quartz, July 24, 2017, https://qz.com/1036163/ubers-least-popular-feature-is-now-all-over-food-delivery-apps.

9. Griswold, "Uber's Least Popular Feature."

10. Griswold, "Uber's Least Popular Feature."

11. Giccariello-Maher, "My Best Friend Lost His Life to the Gig Economy."

Index

About the Author

Saru Jayaraman is the co-founder of the Restaurant Opportunities Centers United, director of the Food Labor Research Center at the University of California, Berkeley, and the author of *Behind the Kitchen Door* and *Forked: A New Standard for American Dining.*

Publishing in the Public Interest

Thank you for reading this book published by The New Press. The New Press is a nonprofit, public interest publisher. New Press books and authors play a crucial role in sparking conversations about the key political and social issues of our day.

We hope you enjoyed this book and that you will stay in touch with The New Press. Here are a few ways to stay up to date with our books, events, and the issues we cover:

- Sign up at www.thenewpress.com/subscribe to receive updates on New Press authors and issues and to be notified about local events
- Like us on Facebook: www.facebook.com/newpress books
- Follow us on Twitter: www.twitter.com/thenewpress
- Follow us on Instagram: www.instagram.com/the newpress

Please consider buying New Press books for yourself; for friends and family; or to donate to schools, libraries, community centers, prison libraries, and other organizations involved with the issues our authors write about.

The New Press is a 501(c)(3) nonprofit organization. You can also support our work with a tax-deductible gift by visiting www.thenewpress.com/donate.